ANCIENT EGYPT

Kingdom of the Pharaohs

ANCIENT EGYPT

Kingdom of the Pharaohs

R. Hamilton

p

This is a Parragon Publishing Book
This edition published in 2005

Parragon Publishing
Queen Street House
4 Queen Street
Bath
BA1 1HE, UK

All photographs © Werner Forman Archive
(see page 256 for full details)
Text © Parragon 2005

Produced by Atlantic Publishing

ISBN 1-40545-057-6

Printed in China

Contents

Introduction

November 26th 1922 saw not only the greatest find since the birth of Egyptology but the most spectacular archeological discovery ever. When Howard Carter stepped into the tomb of Tutankhamun he found a cache of extraordinary treasures untouched for over 3000 years. The world marveled at the funerary goods buried with the boy-king, including the famous solid gold death mask. And yet, prior to Carter's discovery little was known of this relatively minor Eighteenth Dynasty pharaoh, whose tomb was almost certainly a hastily chosen late substitute. If the Tutankhamun treasure was magnificent, what would the tombs of the great Old Kingdom pharaohs have revealed had they not been plundered in antiquity?

Carter's spectacular discovery—spiced with media tales of the mummies' revenge—brought Egyptology from the rarefied realms of academia to the masses. But for those who had made unlocking the secrets of this ancient civilization a lifetime study, it was not Tutankhamun's curse which put the subject on the map; it was a breakthrough which had occurred a century earlier.

In 1822 Jean Francois Champollion finally succeeded in deciphering the hieroglyphs inscribed on the Rosetta Stone, a slab of basalt discovered by a

French soldier twenty-three years earlier. Across Europe there was already a huge revival of interest in learning about the land of the pharaohs, particularly following the publication of *Description de l'Egypte*. This vast work, published in twenty volumes over two decades, was the fruit of Napoleon Bonaparte's military and cultural expedition, mounted in 1798. Militarily it was a complete failure; but experts in every field conducted painstaking research into all facets of Egyptian culture, including the remarkable achievements of the Pharaonic era. *Description de l'Egypte* helped create a thirst for knowledge of this ancient civilization; and simultaneously, Champollion provided the key to understanding the only form of writing in use for the entire Pharaonic period, a key which had been lost for over a thousand years.

Of course, it did not require the birth of Egyptology to unearth the single most enduring image associated with the period: the iconic pyramid. In their day the Old Kingdom tombs were the greatest civil engineering projects on the planet, and remain remarkable technological achievements even by twenty-first-century standards.

Yet Egypt under the pharaohs was far more than simply a country blessed with vast wealth and marvelous craftsmen. This was a society with a particular world view, and its achievements and practices were informed by a powerful set of beliefs.

The Egyptians believed that at the point of creation order emerged from chaos. The universe remained in delicate balance, and the preservation of harmony was a continuing preoccupation. It was the primary responsibility of the pharaoh to maintain order, both within the body politic and in the entire universe. It was his duty to ensure the constancy of the sun and the Nile, the two great life-giving forces. This was achieved by an act of reciprocity. The semi-divine king acted as intermediary between the people and the gods; if the latter were propitiated, order was maintained and a bountiful existence guaranteed.

Egyptian theology developed directly from daily experience. Unsurprisingly, in an agricultural society animals played a prominent role. Rams and cows were revered for their virility, crocodiles and snakes feared as bringers of chaos. Creatures were imbued with divine

Below: The Saqqara tomb of Mereruka, chief justice and vizier during the reign of the Sixth Dynasty king Teti. Mereruka married the king's eldest daughter, enhancing his status still further. The tomb lies adjacent to Teti's pyramid, in accordance with the convention of relatives and important officials being interred in the environs of the king's burial complex.

powers and linked to particular deities; and ultimately they were believed to be the earthly incarnation of those gods. In turn, the hundreds of deities were used to explain the world. For example, when it was discovered that five extra days were needed to bring the 360-day Egyptian calendar in line with the solar year, an entire mythology involving a rift between the gods was invented to account for the discrepancy.

Egypt was a highly stratified society, with the pharaoh at the apex. Individuals bore little envy or resentment towards those above them in the social order, for two main reasons. First, even those at the lower end of the social scale felt privileged to be able to enjoy an ordered existence in a land of plenty. Second, through fulfilling their allotted role, all Egyptians believed they would secure their place in a glorious afterlife. These tenets underpinned Egyptian society for three millennia. There were periods of great turbulence and upheaval, yet

Above: Abusir, one of the royal necropolises which served Memphis, Egypt's first capital after the country was unified c. 3100 BC. Sahure, the second king of the Fifth Dynasty, was the first ruler to choose Abusir as the site for his pyramid complex, a pattern followed by

several of his successors. The reliefs in the Abusir tombs are magnificently executed, but the pyramids themselves are less impressive than their Fourth Dynasty counterparts at Giza. They are on a smaller scale and the core consisted of bonded rubble instead of solid stone.

there was a fundamental stasis which endured in Egypt longer than any other civilization, either before or since.

Advanced and innovative in so many ways, the Egyptians were also instinctively conservative. Whether in construction, transport, medicine or agriculture, once a system was developed that worked, they saw no need to change. For example, the Nile was their motorway, which could be traversed easily by boat. And so there was no need for a highway system or wheeled transport; there seems to have been no Egyptian word for "bridge," They were also an insular people, and not just by dint of geographical circumstance. Self-sufficient as far as basic needs went, the Egyptians were wary of foreigners. The Egyptian word for "mankind" was *remeth*, which also meant Egyptians!

Economically strong, scientifically advanced, culturally rich: such were the hallmarks of the the Pharaonic age, a glorious 3000-year period in which the god-kings of thirty-one dynasties presided over a sophisticated people responsible for some breathtaking achievements. Much has been learned in the two centuries since the birth of Egyptology, but the picture is far from complete. Fresh discoveries add to the corpus of knowledge each year, and the fact that experts sometimes interpret the evidence in different ways only serves to heighten the fascination. The study of Ancient Egypt is thus an unfolding drama, not a finished act. It is a civilization which continues to excite and inspire, a perennial source of wonder and mystery.

Time Line

Predynastic Period
(c. 5500 BC–c. 3100 BC)

Climatic changes render delta region and Nile valley habitable. Rich silt deposits left by annual inundation make for abundant crop yields. Transition from hunter-gatherers to settled agricultural communities takes place. Over time these unite, either for security or economic reasons. Larger political entities brings theological amalgamation as local gods are merged or assimilated. Eventually two kingdoms emerge, and around 3100 BC the delta region of Lower Egypt is subsumed within the realm of Upper Egypt, creating a unified land. Narmer becomes first ruler of the Dynastic era, his deeds recorded on the Narmer Palette.

The death–rebirth cycle of the two great natural forces, the sun and the Nile, informs the Egyptians' view regarding mortality in the physical world and an idyllic existence in the afterlife. Mastaba tombs appear for the elite classes and funerary rituals develop, including interring the dead with an elaborate range of grave goods.

Hieroglyphs develop c. 3400 BC, possibly adapting the idea from Mesopotamian cuneiform script.

Early Dynastic Period
(c. 3100 BC–c. 2686 BC
First and Second Dynasties)

The capital and royal court are based at Memphis, with Abydos as the main necropolis. Development of bureaucratic structures which form the template for the later Pharaonic era. Ideas relating to kingship established, the incumbent not only enjoying absolute secular power as Ruler of the Two Lands but also identified with the gods as the earthly embodiment of Horus. Increasing prominence of the Sun God Re in the pantheon, and "Son of Re" becomes part of the royal titulary. Calendar based on astral movement devised. Development of hieratic script.

Old Kingdom
(c. 2686 BC–c. 2181 BC
Third–Sixth Dynasties)

First great period of the Pharaonic era. Egypt becomes a sophisticated society, technologically advanced and culturally rich. Pyramid construction becomes the pre-eminent state project, the Egyptians believing that their place in a bountiful afterlife dependent on the splendor of the king's funerary monument. Djoser's Step Pyramid, the first to be built in stone, built at Saqqara, the brainchild of his vizier Imhotep. The first true pyramid appears in the Fourth Dynasty, the peak of this architectural form. Khufu, Khafre, and Menkaure build pyramids at Giza, on which site the Great Sphinx is also constructed. Fifth Dynasty pyramids more modest as magnificent sun temples are built in addition to burial complexes. First appearance of Pyramid Texts. The death of the Sixth Dynasty ruler Pepy II precipitates a period of decline as royal wealth and authority diminishes. Provincial nobles wield increasing power and vie for supremacy. Incursions from Asiatics add to a state of chaos in the body politic.

First Intermediate Period
(c. 2181 BC–c. 2055 BC
Seventh–Eleventh Dynasties)

Period of disunity and instability, with royal authority undermined and provincial rulers fighting for power. Political fragmentation brings economic hardship and famine. Seventh and Eighth Dynasties see a succession of

brief, possibly concurrent, reigns, and these kings may not have ruled over the entire country. Decline in royal authority leads all strata of society to secure a place in the afterlife individually. Rise in prominence of Osiris, the mythical slain king who was resurrected to become king of the Underworld. Rulers originating from Herakleopolis gain ascendancy in Ninth Dynasty. Conflict with Theban princes, who gain either a military or diplomatic victory. Mentuhotep II founds Eleventh Dynasty. Royal court moves to Thebes. Order and prosperity restored.

Middle Kingdom
(c. 2055 BC–c. 1650 BC
Eleventh–Fourteenth Dynasties)

Second great era of prosperity and achievement. Regarded as the golden age of literature, and all arts and crafts reach dazzling heights. Amenemhat I usurps throne to found Twelfth Dynasty and introduces coregency to forestall future coups. Itjtawy becomes the new capital. Amun elevated in the pantheon and temple at Karnak established, though Osiris now the pre-eminent deity and Abydos the most important pilgrimage center. Return to pyramid-building, though not on Old Kingdom scale. Coffin Texts, derived from the Old Kingdom Pyramid

future invasion. Egypt becomes more expansionist, with campaigns in Palestine and Syria. Tuthmosis III becomes Egypt's greatest warrior-king. Rise in the cult of the solar deity the Aten reaches a peak under Amenhotep IV, who proscribes all other gods, changes his name to Akhenaten,

Texts, become part of burial ritual. Nubia annexed. Late Twelfth Dynasty brings new period of decline. Itjtawy abandoned. Migrant Middle East group the Hyksos settle in Egypt. Bronze-smelting developed.

Second Intermediate Period
(c. 1650 BC–c. 1550 BC Fifteenth–Seventeenth Dynasties)

Central power again eroded. During Fifteenth and Sixteenth Dynasties the reigns of indigenous rulers run concurrently with those of the Hyksos, who establish a capital at Avaris in the delta. Hyksos rulers assume pharaoh's role, taking on traditional royal duties as well as enjoying the privileges of kingship. They bring new ideas and technology in weaponry, construction, arts, and crafts. The horse and chariot, lyre and lute appear in Egypt for the first time. During the Seventeenth Dynasty the Hyksos rule from Thebes. Increasing tension with native population leads to insurrection led by Theban princes. Ahmose I succeeds in driving the Hyksos out and founds the Eighteenth Dynasty.

New Kingdom
(c. 1550 BC–c. 1069 BC Eighteenth–Twentieth Dynasties)

Expulsion of the Hyksos restores unity and brings new period of prosperity and power. Victory attributed to Theban god Amun, who becomes pre-eminent deity, a position further enhanced after syncretization with Re to form Amun-Re. Professional army raised to forestall

and relocates royal court to site near modern Tell el-Amarna. Traditional pantheon restored under Tutankhamun. During the Nineteenth Dynasty, founded by the military commander Rameses I, Qantir becomes the capital. Attempted invasions by Libyans, Sea Peoples and Nubians. During the Twentieth Dynasty the Valley of the Kings at Thebes established as the royal necropolis. Late Ramessid period sees economic hardship, civil unrest, and decline in royal authority.

Third Intermediate Period
(c. 1069 BC–c. 747 BC Twenty-first–Twenty-fourth Dynasties)

Smendes founds Twenty-first Dynasty, ruling from Tanis in the delta, while High Priests of Amun rule southern Egypt from Thebes. Intermarriage between the two lines helps the rival factions reach accommodation. Sheshonq I, of Libyan descent, founds Twenty-second Dynasty. Protracted period in which kings of rival dynasties reign concurrently. Rulers from Sais in the delta emerge as dominant line and come closest to reuniting the country.

Piy, ruler of a southern kingdom whose capital was Napata, campaigns as far north as Memphis. Introduction of ironworking.

Late Period (c. 747 BC–c. 332 BC Twenty-fifth–Thirtieth Dynasties)

Napatan leader Shabaqo conquers whole of Egypt to found the Kushite Twenty-fifth Dynasty. Assyrians gain victory over Napatans in 671 BC and establish a Saite line to rule over Egypt. Rise of Babylonian Empire, which defeats the Assyrians in 626 BC. In 525 BC Persia, the new dominant power, invades to found the Twenty-seventh Dynasty. Native insurrection finally results in expulsion of Persians

by Saite leader Amyrtaios. Throne usurped by line from delta city of Mendes to found Twenty-ninth Dynasty. Nectanebo I seizes power to establish Thirtieth Dynasty before Persia's reconquest of Egypt. In 332 BC Alexander the Great invades Egypt, which falls under Greek control.

Graeco-Roman Period (332 BC–AD 641)

Macedonian rule welcomed by Egyptians, who regard Alexander as an enlightened overlord freeing them from the Persian yoke. Alexandria founded as Egypt's new capital. Rule of the Ptolemies, a line descended from one of Alexander the Great's generals. Period of great temple-building as successive kings assume role of pharaoh. Punitive taxation prompts series of rebellions. Decree commemorating the coronation of Ptolemy V in 196 BC inscribed on a basalt slab, later known as the Rosetta Stone. The Ptolemaic line ends with Cleopatra VII, daughter of Ptolemy XII, who unsuccessfully tries to prevent Egypt from becoming a vassal state of Rome. Egypt conquered 30 BC by Octavian and becomes part of Roman Empire. Roman law introduced, though Greek remains the official language. Egypt's main function as granary for Rome. Harsh conditions for native population lead to many attempted rebellions. Spread of Christianity during reign of Constantine I (AD 306–337), and it subsequently becomes Egypt's official religion. Roman rule ends with conquest by Arabs in AD 641. Islam became the predominant religion, though Christianity continues to flourish in the Coptic Church, as it does to this day.

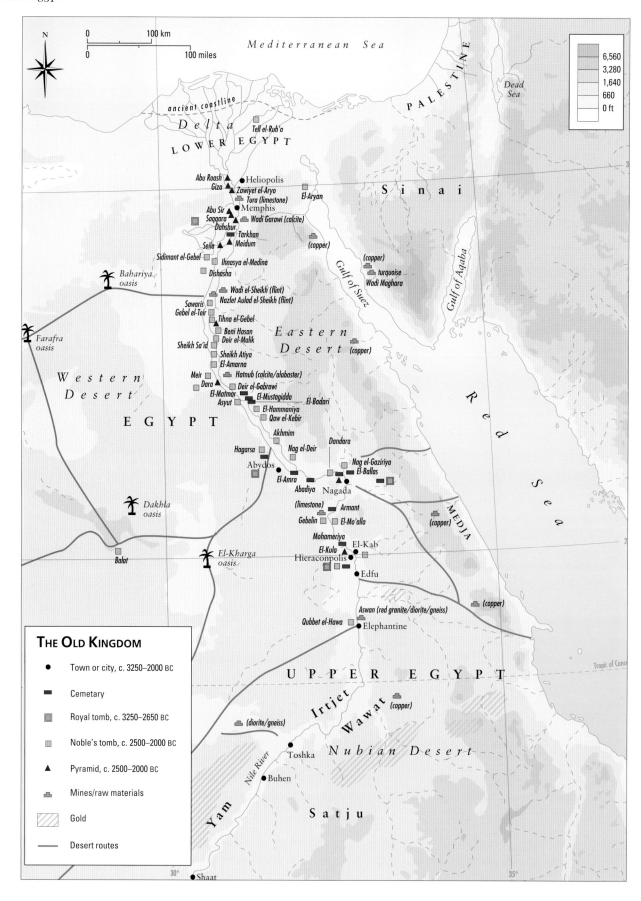

The Old Kingdom map

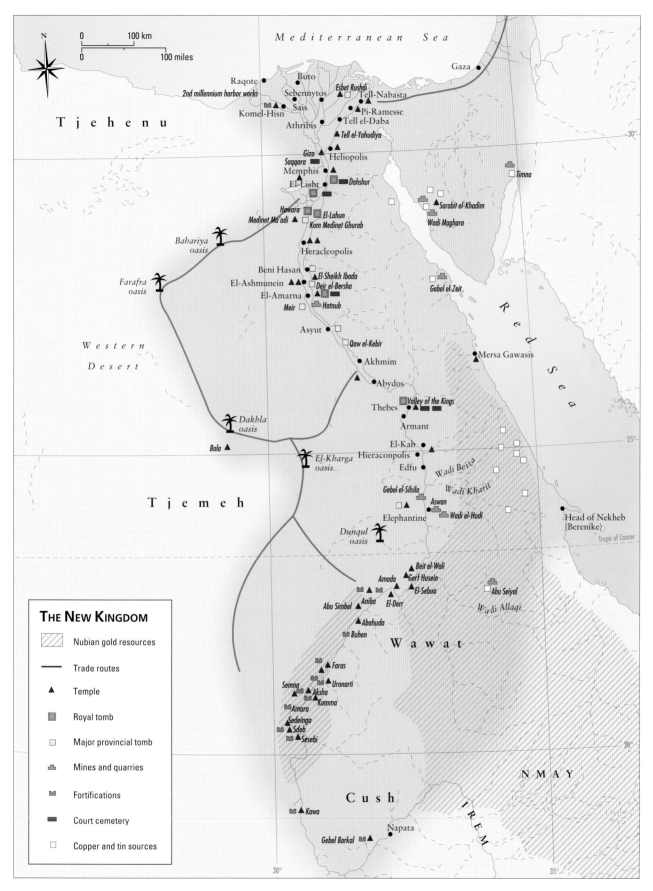

CHAPTER ONE

Birth of a Golden Civilization
c. 3300–2686 BC

There is evidence of human occupation in Egypt as long ago as 200,000 BC. These would have been nomadic hunter-gatherers. In the period following the end of the last Ice Age, around 10,000 BC, agrarian communities started to emerge, although this development was by no means unique to Egypt. The people began to harness the fecundity of the land adjacent to the River Nile, and a degree of settlement gradually took place. Villages sprang up in Upper Egypt—the river valley in the south—and Lower Egypt, the delta area to the north. The terms Upper and Lower were relative to the flow of the Nile, an indication that the river was to be the central factor in the birth of an extraordinary civilization.

All benefited from the rich dark silt deposits which were left following the Nile's annual inundation, and which gave the country its name: Kemet, "the Black Land." Beyond this narrow fertile strip there was vast desert on three sides which was called Deshret, "the Red Land." The harshness of this environment, next to such a beneficent one, was also useful for it provided a natural barrier to hostile outsiders. The Nile also served as a communications highway: boats were first made from the papyrus which grew in plentiful supply on the delta, and later from wood. In short, the geography of the country provided a bountiful food supply, a degree of security, and an efficient transport system, conditions which the indigenous population used to its advantage and which attracted migrants from places such as Syria, Palestine, and Nubia.

The Predynastic Period

Egypt in 5000 BC remained a country of disparate peoples. Skeletal remains show that the inhabitants in the north and south were physically distinct. Upper and Lower Egypt looked to different gods for protection and had their own sacred symbols, the lotus flower and papyrus respectively. A unified political entity was still some 2000 years away, but with their shared experience of life beside the Nile there was probably as much a sense of commonality as difference.

The Predynastic period did give rise to several elements characteristic of the Pharaonic era. Efficient agricultural practices brought prosperity, allowing the people to engage in increasingly sophisticated forms of cultural expression. Craftsmen fashioned jewelry and pottery, and trade routes for such goods became established. Egypt's rich gold deposits were also highly prized by trading partners which included Syria, Lebanon, and Palestine. Increasing affluence inevitably brought social stratification. The burial sites from this period clearly delineate the wealthiest members of society, for it was customary for the deceased to be interred with his or her possessions.

Predynastic Egyptians believed in the afterlife and funerary rituals were well established. Bodies were shrouded and laid out, the sand acting as a natural desiccant and preserver. They were placed facing

Opposite: The Narmer Palette depicts scenes of conquest which are thought to have led to the unification of Egypt c. 3100 BC. Until then the peoples of the north and south of the country had different traditions and were wary of each other, although all

believed that they were fortunate to live in a land of plenty whose benefactor was the bountiful Nile. Indeed the geography of the land—Upper Egypt referred to the south and Lower Egypt the north—was defined by the flow of the river.

west, the direction of the sun's disappearance. As in all contemporary cultures the movement of the sun was a powerful symbol of death and rebirth. The Sun God, Re, became the most important of the many deities the Egyptians worshipped.

The Naqada Period

A new culture was ushered in around 4000 BC. The Naqada period—taking its name from the place in Upper Egypt—lasted some 900 years. Its latter stage is often referred to as the Protodynastic era, the transitional phase between the old order and the founding of the first of the

thirty-one royal dynasties. The early Naqada period was similar to its predecessor in that the people cultivated the land, hunted and fished. However, the remains of mud huts suggest that they lived in at least semi-permanent dwellings, whereas their forebears appear still to have lived something of a nomadic lifestyle.

During the latter part of the Naqada period large-scale immigration occurred in Upper Egypt, in the south of the country. Where these sophisticated newcomers came from is unclear, but it seems that their arrival may have been a catalyst in the creation of a unified state. Graves of kings have been unearthed at Abydos, and with a single ruler in place in the south it is hardly surprising that acquisitive eyes should have been turned northwards. However, conquest may not have been the only factor in uniting the land. Adverse climatic changes and population growth have also been suggested as possible reasons for Egypt falling under centralized control. Efficient husbanding of resources and the undertaking of large-scale infrastructure projects would have been more readily achieved with Egypt as a political and thus bureaucratic entity.

The First Kings

With fertile land at stake and tribal forces at work, it seems likely that alliances and enmities were forged. The degree to which the unification of the country came about as a result of co-operation or conflict remains a matter of speculation; what is clear is that by around 3100 BC Egypt was an extremely sophisticated, highly stratified country with a single ruler.

Left: Statuette said to come from Naqada and known as "MacGregor Man", after the Reverend William MacGregor in whose collection it was until 1922. The makers of early Predynastic sculptures knew as yet none of the conventions of later Egyptian art. This results in the curiously un-Egyptian impression their creations exert.

Opposite: A detail dating from the Eighteenth Dynasty from the tomb of Nakt depicting the gathering of grapes from an arbor.

Legend has it that Menes led the armies of Upper Egypt to victory in the north and became the first king of the unified land, founding the first dynasty and establishing a capital at Memphis. There is no evidence that Menes existed, although the Egyptian priest and historian Manetho, writing in the third century BC, records him as the first dynastic ruler. Two figures for whose existence the evidence is much stronger are Scorpion and Narmer. Scorpion was one of the last kings of the Protodynastic period. A mace-head dating from around 3100 BC shows him wearing the White Crown, symbol of Upper Egypt.

One of the most important extant artifacts relating to this period of flux is the Narmer Palette. This mudstone tablet shows Narmer bearing the same ceremonial crown as Scorpion, and his name is recorded in the hieroglyphs. The obverse of the Palette shows Narmer again, this time wearing the bucket-shaped Red Crown, symbol of Lower Egypt. He is portrayed surveying rows of decapitated corpses in what appears to be a victory parade. As first wearer of the double crown Narmer is usually accorded the status of Egypt's first dynastic ruler. However, the scenes depicted on the Narmer Palette may be symbolic, or show an established order rather than the events of actual conquest. Narmer and Menes may have been one and the same person, or Menes may be a mythical figure whose warringexploits are a conflation of those of Narmer and Scorpion.

The First Dynasty lasted some 200 years, though little is known for certain. There is even doubt about the exact royal lineage of this period, which may have included a queen acting as regent while her son, Den, gained majority. Why this dynasty petered out around 2890 BC is also shrouded in mystery. Information surrounding the seven kings who reigned during the course of the Second Dynasty (c. 2890–c. 2686) is equally sketchy.

The Early Dynastic Period

Archaeological studies, notably by the renowned Egyptologist Sir William Petrie in the late nineteenth century, shed considerable light on the Early Dynastic period. Burial sites discovered at Abydos and Saqqara gave an insight into the funerary rituals of the time and the gods that were worshipped. Tomb construction was modest; it would be several centuries before the great pyramid builders got to work. And yet these early "mastaba" tombs (from the Arabic word for "bench") show that the Egyptians developed clear ideas regarding the journey to the afterlife. Built of mudbrick, these early mastabas vary in scale, reflecting the status of the individual. The royal tombs were naturally the grandest, those of the king's officials being of a more rudimentary design. In some cases it appears that acolytes were murdered to accompany their ruler on the final journey. This practice did not survive long, for the Egyptians believed that models were as effective as the real thing. During the Old Kingdom – the Third to Sixth Dynasties –

Above: A detail from a wall painting in the tomb of Menna in West Thebes dating from the Eighteenth Dynasty. It shows the harvesting of wheat with one worker stacking grain, one resting, while a third plays the flute. Vast surpluses of emmer wheat were stored in silos to insure against the occasional poor harvest. While the Egyptians were great innovators, once an effective method was established it generally endured, and agricultural practices came into this category.

models of servants, known as *shabtis*, were placed in the burial chamber. These would be reanimated by magic spells to tend to their master's needs. Models of food were also deposited to provide sustenance. This was a culture in which understanding of and achievements in science, medicine, and engineering coexisted happily with belief in magic spells and lucky charms.

The riches with which the kings were buried were an irresistible lure from the earliest times. Tombs of the Early Dynastic era were sealed from above, but latterly staircases were incorporated into the design. This allowed the tomb to be constructed before interment, but it also meant an access point for grave-robbers. Portcullises were used as a deterrent, but it is clear that some Ancient Egyptians, out of either greed or necessity, were prepared to risk secular or deific retribution for the prize on offer. This would be a recurring theme over the next three millennia.

Another practice established during the Early Dynastic period was the construction of a building separate from the tomb itself where offerings to the dead king could be made. Such buildings were probably forerunners to the mortuary temples which were built adjacent to the pyramids. As well as being the place where cult offerings could be made, these temples housed the deceased's *ka*, a spirit force which was believed to survive death. The *ka* had to be provided with daily sustenance for the dead person's well-being in the afterlife. Statues of the *ka* were erected, and priests used these to draw the spirit back so that it could receive food and drink.

Inscribed slabs, or stelae, in the tombs of Early Dynastic kings show the importance attributed to the deities and the forms they took. Many were portrayed as animals, or half-human, half-animal. The falcon or hawk represented Horus, who appears repeatedly at these early burial sites. Horus was the son of Osiris, an Egyptian king who, according to legend, was murdered by his brother Seth. Osiris's body was cut into pieces by Seth, who was anxious to claim the crown for himself. Osiris's sister, Isis, gathered the pieces and restored him to life, when he became king of the Underworld. The throne thus remained vacant but Seth was prevented from securing it by Horus, a son born to Osiris and Isis.

Kingship

Egyptian kings were believed to be the living embodiment of Horus, and also son of the most important of all the deities, the Sun God Re. When the ruler died he passed into the land of the dead to be reunited with Re, while his successor became the new Horus. Egyptian rulers were thus regarded as divine, or at least as an intermediary between the mortal world and the gods. One of the most important of the king's duties was to appease the deities

through ritualistic offerings, thereby ensuring that order and prosperity were maintained. Similarly, the king was often depicted smiting a foe or quelling a wild beast, both of which were seen as threats to the harmonious cycle of the Egyptian calendar. In Egyptian mythology Seth represented chaos of any kind, and the king was the conduit through which this blight was overcome.

The Egyptians had the utmost respect for their ruler. It was common for people at court to kiss the ground before the royal feet. The word "pharaoh"—literally "great house"—refers to the opulence of the royal household but also suggests the awe which ordinary people felt for both the office and its incumbent. This term was not actually applied to the ruler himself for another thousand years, during the New Kingdom era, but the Egyptians' perception of and attitude toward kingship was clearly established in the Early Dynastic period.

Below: A detail of a fragment of the "Battlefield Palette" from the late Predynastic period shows the king as a lion devouring a slain foe, while the bodies of the enemies are strewn over the battlefield.

The royal regalia was suffused with symbolism. The king carried a crook and flail, representing the authority of his office and the fertility of the land respectively. A cobra incorporated into the royal crown was ready to strike at any potential enemy who posed a threat to the king, which was tantamount to an attack on the maintained order. A beard was another symbol of kingship, one which could equally be used in depictions of female pharaohs, though these were few in number. One of the most important of the royal trappings was the *ankh*, the symbol of life. The holder had the power of life and death in his hands and was the exclusive preserve of the ruler and the gods.

Above: A detail showing a griffin and a jackal, or a man wearing a jackal mask, playing the flute, from the "Two Dogs Palette" found at Nekhen (Hierakonpolis). For the Egyptians, the deserts bordering the Nile valley were the home of wild animals and mythical beasts and represented chaos.

Social Structure

Below the king, who stood at the apex of the social pyramid, came members of the royal family, then priests, nobles, advisors, scribes, and officials. The most important civil servant was the vizier, whose role was equivalent to that of chief executive. As the king was head of both religious and secular life, including the legal and financial systems, the army—even regulator of trade and the food supply—delegation was obviously required. The ruler executed his powers through the vizier, who oversaw all departments and reported directly to the king. The Red and White Houses, representing Lower and Upper Egypt respectively, were administered separately.

Beneath the nobles and senior officials came the skilled workers. In their industry the Ancient Egyptians went far beyond mere utilitarianism, prizing luxury goods for use both in the present and the afterlife. Jewellers fashioned gold and semiprecious stones such as amethyst, agate, and turquoise; masons worked a range of types of stone, including alabaster, basalt, and diorite, raising the level of craftsmanship to new heights; skilled carpenters, using increasingly sophisticated tools and techniques on quality imported timber such as cedar and ebony, made furniture, statues, musical instruments, and gaming boards with remarkably intricate detailing. Artisans of all kinds were well regarded and well rewarded, and were often allocated special districts in which to live and work.

By far the greatest proportion of the population, however, was made up of the peasant class, who worked the land according to a rigid annual cycle. The inundation occurred over the summer months and during this time peasant farmers could be co-opted to work on any assigned task. This could have been military service in time of war, and was especially important when great civil engineering projects were being undertaken.

Plowing and sowing took place in the fall. Barley and emmer wheat, the chief grain crops, were harvested in early spring. The produce was stored in silos, and surpluses provided insurance against years when the waters of the Nile rose too high or not high enough, both of which had a catastrophic effect on the harvest.

The peasants' lot was often that of serfdom; they could be bought and sold by the farmers who controlled the estates on which they worked. However, they enjoyed a good diet of bread, pulses, vegetables, fruit, and fish. A thick beer made from barley was the staple drink. A document dating from the Early Dynastic period contended that even the poorest class in Egypt enjoyed a lifestyle akin to that of the wealthiest in any other culture, and it is easy to see why this conjecture may have gained credence. Economically strong and culturally rich, Egypt had embarked on a period of great stability and glittering achievement the like of which has never been seen, either before or since.

By the time the first two dynasties petered out, Egypt was a thriving, efficient, and highly ordered society. The Third Dynasty, which began c. 2690 BC, would see even more spectacular accomplishments. The Old Kingdom, as the next four dynasties are collectively known, lasted some 500 years. This was the age of the pyramid builders, the first great era in a 3000-year golden civilization.

Right: A Second Dynasty (c. 2650 BC) statue of Khasekhem, one of two statues deposited in the temple of Horus in Hierakonpolis. He is wearing a costume associated with jubilee festivals, when the power of the king was renewed.

CHAPTER TWO

Age of the Pyramid Builders
c. 2686–2181 *BC*

By the beginning of the Third Dynasty Egypt was a stratified, centralized country, with the king at the apex of both secular and religious life. The inundation—often described as the Nile's annual gift—provided the wealth for successive rulers to make their mark, and technological developments allowed their vision to be realized. This was the beginning of the Old Kingdom, the first great peak in Egyptian civilization.

Such was the Ancient Egyptians' preoccupation with death as a welcome staging post on the way to a glorious afterlife, it is hardly surprising that funerary practices became increasingly elaborate. During the Old Kingdom the mudbrick mastabas of the previous era were still used for officials but for the kings themselves tomb construction was taken to a breathtaking new level. Decades would be spent on the planning and construction of such tombs, the workforce at times comprising tens of thousands of men. This was the age of the great pyramid builders, the fruits of whose labors provide the single most enduring image associated with Ancient Egypt.

As an architectural form the pyramid—from the Greek "pyramis," meaning "wheat cake," presumably because of its shape—was relatively shortlived. By the end of the Old Kingdom, c. 2150 BC, pyramid construction was in decline. During the New Kingdom era, which began c. 1550 BC, most pharaohs would be buried in the Valley of the Kings, their tombs cut into the hills on the west of the Nile at Thebes. Security may have been one factor. The pyramids, even with the structural deterrents incorporated into their design, fell prey to grave-robbers. Cost may have been another issue: interment in the Valley of the Kings represented a much cheaper option. However, this was a thousand years hence. With the beginning of the Third Dynasty Egyptian kings ordered the construction of some extraordinary burial monuments, spectacular feats of civil engineering which impress and inspire to this day.

The First Pyramids

Little is known of Sanakht, whose brief reign launched the Third Dynasty. His successor, Djoser, is a much more significant figure. He oversaw a great leap forward in tomb construction, one which was logical in terms of both design and symbolic import. As far as design was concerned there was a natural progression from the mastaba, essentially setting increasingly small rectangular layers on top of each other. Djoser's tomb had a base measuring just over 60m square which was then raised to create a six-level stepped monument some 60m high. In terms of symbolism the Step Pyramid was a stairway by which Djoser would have reached the sky and taken his place alongside the gods. It was the largest structure in Egypt at the time, c. 2650 BC, and the first in the world to be built entirely from stone.

Much of the detailing in the design of the tomb complex presents images of more familiar construction materials, wood and reeds. Lotus and papyrus motifs, symbols of Upper and Lower Egypt, are a recurring design theme. That these natural forms were recreated in stone is a testament to the craftsmanship and vision of those who contributed to this remarkable undertaking. It was an extraordinary achievement, the scale of which reflected the status

Opposite: The Pyramids at Giza, one of the Seven Wonders of the Ancient World.

Above: Detail of a wooden stela from the mastaba tomb of Hesire, chief physician and scribe in the reign of King Djoser. High-ranking officials were often buried in the funerary complex of the ruler they served. Hesire's tomb was built near Djoser's Step Pyramid at Saqqara.

accorded to an Egyptian ruler. On a more practical level the Step Pyramid was also a feat of industry and organization. It may have been used as a means of focusing the minds and efforts of a vast workforce, providing a common purpose to maintain order.

Djoser's pyramid was built at Saqqara, to the west of Memphis, which was an important necropolis for Egyptian kings and high-ranking officials right up to the New Kingdom era. It is housed within a much larger walled complex the size of a town. There are functional buildings, for example those associated with the cult practices honoring the dead king. There are also dummy buildings, whose purpose appears to be simply to recreate Memphis, the first capital of the united land. Just as Egyptians provided dummy food and *shabti* model servants to service the needs of the king in the afterlife, so it seems that Djoser was provided with an entire urban domain over which to preside.

The complex also includes the *heb sed* court. *Heb sed* was a jubilee festival, usually held to celebrate thirty years on the throne, in which the king's royal prerogative was renewed. The fact that this was part of the tomb complex emphasizes the fact that the Egyptians believed such a ceremony applied equally to the mortal world and the afterlife.

The Step Pyramid was the brainchild of Djoser's vizier, Imhotep, who was also a doctor, scribe, priest, and astronomer, serving under four kings. Imhotep's remarkable talents were acknowledged in the Late Egyptian period, some 2000 years after his death, when he was worshiped in his own right as a god of medicine.

Djoser's mortuary temple is situated at the north face of the pyramid. Such temples would soon be relocated to the eastern face, allowing for a direct causeway connection to the Nile. Such causeways were used to transport materials from the river to the pyramid sites. When construction was complete a valley temple was built on the site where causeway and river met.

The final east–west journey across the Nile was deeply symbolic, mirroring the sun's journey through the sky. In the valley temples purification rituals were performed which revived the dead king's spirit before he took his place among the gods. Once again the imagery of death and rebirth was powerful: the Egyptians believed that the Sun God Re was reborn daily by bathing in a sacred lake.

The Fourth Dynasty

The Third Dynasty came to an end with the reign of Huni, although there may have been a familial connection with the first Fourth Dynasty king, Sneferu. Both may have contributed toward the next important development in pyramid construction: smooth-faced sides instead of steps. The pyramid at Meidum, the building of which may have begun during Huni's reign, was also conceived as a stepped design. The sides were subsequently filled in, possibly on Sneferu's instructions, to provide the first instance of true pyramid construction. In doing so the design concept of the stairway to the skies was obviously lost. However, the shape of the true pyramid was thought to represent the sun's rays falling on earth. The king was believed to ascend to the heavens on these rays, and so the change in pyramid design merely reflected a different symbolical mode of transport for the king's final journey to join the deities.

The Meidum Pyramid today is a three-stepped edifice atop a mass of rubble. It is unclear whether it fell into disrepair as a result of later human activity or whether it was abandoned in an unfinished state. The case for the latter is strengthened by the fact that the stelae in the mortuary chapel are not inscribed with the king's name. As the Egyptians were fervent believers in posthumous rituals which preserved the name and spirit of past rulers, it seems likely that the Meidum Pyramid is associated with Sneferu's reign but not his journey to the afterlife.

Sneferu ordered the construction of two more pyramids, at Dahshur, giving further credence to the theory that the Meidum project was aborted. Again these were both smooth-sided, but one has two angles of elevation. Its faces emerge from the ground at one angle, then halfway up there is a change to a shallower angle as it rises to its apex. The so-called "Bent Pyramid" may have been a design experiment or there may have been concerns that to continue building at the original steeper angle ran the risk of collapse in unstable ground conditions. The Bent Pyramid is certainly dedicated to Sneferu, although its near neighbor, known as the Red Pyramid, may have been the king's final resting place. The latter is a true pyramid and gets its popular name from the iron oxide present in the stone, which gives it its distinctive hue.

The Meidum Pyramid and the two associated with Sneferu at Dahshur saw another interesting development. In each case the tomb chamber was in the heart of the pyramid rather than beneath it. This required the use of corbeled roofs on the chambers to support the enormous weight above.

In terms of scale, pyramid-building reached its zenith during the reign of Sneferu's successor, his son Khufu. He oversaw the construction of the Great Pyramid at Giza, the only one of the Seven Wonders of the Ancient World still in existence. Nearby are the pyramids of Khafre and Menkaure, two later Fourth Dynasty kings. Each of the three complexes follows a similar pattern: there are smaller pyramids for the royal wives and mastabas for senior court officials and relatives; the mortuary temple, adjacent to the pyramid, is linked to the valley temple by a causeway; and there is a channel connecting the latter to the waters of the Nile.

Preservation of the Body

Khufu's burial chamber did not survive intact but that of his mother, Hetepheres I, chief wife of Sneferu, was unearthed in 1925. Hetepheres was interred in a deep-shaft tomb on the eastern side of the Great Pyramid. Although the sarcophagus was empty, an alabaster chest containing her internal organs was found. This proves that advances in preservation techniques had been made by the time of the Fourth Dynasty. The Egyptians used natron, a sodium compound, as a cleansing and desiccating agent. They had obviously discovered that the internal organs would cause the body to decay from within, no matter how effectively it had been preserved

Below: Detail from the internal wall of the mastaba of Nefermaat at Meidum, where some of the finest examples of Fourth Dynasty tomb paintings were discovered.

externally with resin-soaked strips of linen. The practice of organ removal began, and even here a precise ritual was eventually established. They were stored in canopic jars, whose figure-shaped stoppers were associated with particular deities and offered protection. The stoppers took the form of a human head, and the heads of an ape, jackal, and falcon, housing the liver, lungs, stomach, and intestines respectively. However, canopic jars in this form did not come into widespread use until around 1500 BC. Although the Egyptians' knowledge of anatomy and medicine was advanced in many ways, the brain was regarded as superfluous tissue with no useful function, and it was removed via the nasal cavity. The heart, on the other hand, was seen as the organ which governed reason, emotion, and personality traits. It was left in place for a judgement ceremony before Osiris known as the Weighing of the Heart. The heart was placed on a pair of scales and weighed against a feather, representing truth. If the weight of misdeeds caused the balance to tip in the heart's favor the person would not be granted passage to the afterlife. In such cases the organ would be devoured by Ammut, a ferocious beast with a crocodile's head, a lion's forelegs, and the hindquarters of a hippopotamus.

The Sphinx

Khufu was succeeded by Djedefre, whose brief reign, together with the fact that he built his own monument at Abu Roash to the north of Giza, has led to speculation that there was a rift which may have resulted in a coup. Khafre, son of Khufu and half-brother to Djedefre, came to the throne c. 2558 BC. Khafre's pyramid at Giza appears bigger than Khufu's, an illusion created by the fact that it was built on higher ground. Near Khafre's valley temple, facing east toward the rising sun, stands that other great icon of the era, the Sphinx. The head, which bears the royal nemes headcloth, is believed to have been fashioned in Khafre's image. This great stone monument which guards the entire Giza complex has the body of a lion, a symbol of the king's power. The lion was also associated with Re, reinforcing the connection between the earthly ruler and the deities.

There were long periods when the Sphinx was covered in sand. The inscribed stela between the lion's paws tells the story of Tuthmosis, who fell asleep there and was promised in a dream that he would become pharaoh if he cleared the sand away and carried out repairs to the monument. He did so and acceded to the throne as Tuthmosis IV, c. 1400 BC.

Opposite: Scribes were part of the élite in Ancient Egyptian society. They were not simply clerical workers but senior officials involved in all aspects of government. In artwork scribes were invariably portrayed sitting cross-legged with a papyrus scroll on their knees.

Giza

Menkaure, son of Khafre, came to the throne c. 2532 BC and instituted work on the third pyramid complex at Giza. It is much smaller than its neighbors, possibly because Menkaure wanted it cased in costly material. The lower facade is of red granite but this was abandoned after sixteen courses. It is possible that Menkaure died before construction was complete and his son, Shepseskaf, finished the job in mudbrick. Shepseskaf himself opted for a mastaba tomb, large but modest compared to the great pyramids. The trend had turned toward less spectacular royal burial sites, perhaps on grounds of economy, or perhaps because it was felt that an undue amount of time and resources was being spent on the king's tomb compared with that spent worshiping and appeasing the gods.

The Fifth Dynasty

The Fourth Dynasty ended with Shepseskaf, although events surrounding the transition to the Fifth Dynasty are unclear. Several of the Fifth Dynasty kings were buried at Abusir, south of Giza. Userkaf, founder of this royal line, had his pyramid built at Saqqara, with a sun temple at Abusir. The latter place became established as the main necropolis for this dynasty. These pyramids are smaller in scale than their Fourth Dynasty counterparts, although the quality remained impressive. The practice of building sun temples in honour of Re in addition to pyramids continued throughout the Fifth Dynasty and the very fact that the kings were undertaking two major projects instead of one may account for the more modest scale of pyramid construction. It was in this period that the cult of the Sun God reached its zenith. The creation myth surrounding Re, which centered on Heliopolis, seems to have assumed even greater importance during this period. Six kings are known to have built sun temples near Abusir, all based on the earliest known example, which was constructed at Heliopolis c. 2600 BC. Kings also adopted the title "Sa Re"—Son of the Sun God— further consolidating the connection between the earthly ruler and the divine.

Unas

The Fifth Dynasty came to an end with the reign of Unas (c. 2375–c. 2345). Little is known of his reign, and his pyramid at Saqqara is the smallest built during the Old Kingdom, yet Unas is a significant figure, the first known king to have the internal walls of his pyramid inscribed with spells. These insured that no harm came to the king on his journey to the afterlife. Known as the

Pyramid Texts, these writings would be a feature of burial rituals for the next three dynasties. On the causeway linking Unas's valley and mortuary temples are many reliefs depicting varied scenes, presumably associated with the king's reign. Among them are images of emaciated figures, suggesting that there may have been a famine. Whether this affected Egypt itself or a neighboring land to which Unas benevolently gave assistance is uncertain. However, the fact that the Old Kingdom would come to an end when the Sixth Dynasty petered out suggests a period of decline had set in.

Decline of the Old Kingdom

The transition between the Fifth and Sixth Dynasties is again unclear, although there is evidence that these were turbulent times. Teti, the new dynasty's first ruler, appears to have been involved in a power struggle with the provincial governors, whose offices became hereditary. The historian Manetho, writing some 2000 years later, claimed that Teti was assassinated. Before his heir, Pepi I, acceded to the throne the shadowy figure of Userkara reigned briefly and it has been suggested that a coup d'état may have taken place. Pepi I made late marriages with two sisters, daughters of an official named Khui. These women bore the next two kings, Merenre and Pepi II, and the fact that Khui's son became vizier during their reigns suggests that Khui himself may have been a powerful figure, assuming the role of éminence grise.

Pepi II came to the throne on the early death of his half-brother. He is reputed to have reigned for ninety-four years, the longest in history. His longevity may have been a factor in the decadence which seems to have precipitated the end of the Old Kingdom. The aging Pepi II is said to have been a hedonist and possibly homosexual. His great age may also have created a succession problem as he could have outlived his natural heirs.

The Old Kingdom came to an end with the short reign of Queen Nitiqret. Folklore whose provenance is nearest to the actual events speaks of widespread crisis and disorder. Turmoil in the body politic, invasion from foreign lands, and failure of the Nile to rise have all been proposed as reasons why the Old Kingdom went into terminal decline and ended c. 2181 BC.

Left: Statue of the Third Dynasty king, Djoser, who reigned c. 2667 BC–2648 BC. He is wearing the nemes headcloth and ceremonial false beard, which were part of the royal regalia. Little is known about Djoser's life but he is remembered for his magnificent funerary monument, the Step Pyramid (previous pages).

Built at Saqqara, an important necropolis to the west of the capital Memphis, the Step Pyramid was a natural development from the low rectangular mastaba tombs which preceded it. It was designed by the celebrated vizier and architect Imhotep, and marked the beginning of a millennium during which such awe-inspiring monuments were built. The Step Pyramid was not just a vast tomb but an entire complex, recreating the city of Memphis for Djoser to preside over in the afterlife. The statue was found in the serdab, *a special chamber for housing the deceased king's ka statue. The ka was a spiritual double which the Egyptians believed continued to live on after death, and which therefore needed daily sustenance.*

Above: The use of colored paste inlays appears to have been a shortlived artistic experiment during the Fourth Dynasty. This example is from the tomb of Nefermaat and Atet at Meidum.

Right: Painted limestone statues of Prince Rahotep— who may have been a son of King Sneferu, founder of the Fourth Dynasty—and his wife Nofret. They were discovered in 1871 in a mastaba tomb near the Meidum Pyramid by French Egyptologist Auguste Mariette. The Meidum Pyramid was conceived as a stepped design but the sides were subsequently filled in to make it the earliest known true pyramid. The project seems to have been abandoned, Sneferu having two farther pyramids built at Dahshur.

Right: The provenance of the Meidum Pyramid is uncertain. It may have belonged to Huni, the last Third Dynasty king, or his son Sneferu, founder of the Fourth. Both may have contributed to its construction, the father instituting the project and the son carrying it on. The fact that there are no inscribed stelae associated with the Meidum Pyramid adds weight to the theory that it was abandoned by Sneferu, whose actual resting place is thought to be the so-called Red Pyramid at Dahshur.

Left: This gilded chair was among the spectacular funerary equipment found in the tomb of Queen Hetepheres I, which was discovered in 1925 near the Great Pyramid of her son, Khufu. All pyramids quickly became a target for thieves but Hetepheres' shaft grave was not unearthed in antiquity and provided some of the best evidence of royal burial practices during the Old Kingdom.

Below: The chapel of the tomb of Meryre-nufer Qar. Meryre-nufer Qar was the "overseer of the pyramid-towns of Khufu and Menkaure", and "inspector of priests of the pyramid of Khephren". He was buried in the old Fourth Dynasty cemetery at Giza. The figures are cut directly into the rock.

Left: In 1954 the first of five boat pits was discovered near Khufu's Great Pyramid. It contained over 1200 pieces of cedar, acacia and other woods, material for a vessel over 40m long and beam of almost 6m. It took experts over a decade to complete this intricate jigsaw puzzle. Similar vessels have been discovered, both before and since, but Khufu's majestic funerary barque remains one of the jewels recovered from the Pharaonic era. It is on display in the Boat Museum at Giza.

Boats played a significant role in Egyptian funerary beliefs. The Sun God Re was believed to travel through the skies and the Underworld by solar barque, and after death the king was thought to embark on a similar journey. Khufu's body may also have been transported on its final journey in this vessel. It thus probably fulfilled both a practical and symbolic function.

Left: The pyramids at Giza, one of the Seven Wonders of the Ancient World. Giza was the most important necropolis for Fourth Dynasty Egyptian kings. Pyramid construction reached its zenith with the tomb complexes of Khufu, his son Khafre, and grandson Menkaure. Khafre's pyramid, center, appears larger than Khufu's Great Pyramid beyond it, an illusion created by the fact that it was built on higher ground. Khafre's pyramid complex is the best preserved of the three, however, in particular the magnificent valley temple dedicated to him. The apex of Khafre's pyramid retains some of its original Tura limestone casing, most of which was removed from the site in the ninth century for construction work in Cairo.

How the Pyramids Were Built

There are no records describing the construction techniques that were employed by the pyramid builders and these have been the subject of much speculation over the years. It was thought that base levels were established by flooding the site with water, but this would have been a colossal undertaking. Current thinking is that water-filled trenches combined with A-frame plumb-bob devices were used to achieve level foundations.

Transporting the huge blocks—which could weigh up to 15 tonnes—from the river to the construction site was probably done on sledges pulled across a rolling road of wooden planks, with water or mud used as a lubricant. This theory has largely supplanted the idea that rollers were employed, as the friction level would have been higher and thus required an even greater force of manpower to overcome it.

Knowledge of astronomy allowed the Egyptians to align the pyramid with the cardinal points. They understood that a 3-4-5 triangle could be used to check for squareness, and the angle of inclination of the sides was maintained using a device called a *seqed*. The north–south axis mirrored the geography of the Nile, the east–west axis the journey of the sun. The orientation of the pyramid thus encapsulated the two most important phenomena which underpinned secular life and theological belief.

How the blocks were raised into position remains open to question, although it is generally accepted that ramps were used. One straight ramp would have been a massive undertaking in its own right and it is now thought that these were used from ground level to around one-third height. From there to the summit a wrap-around ramp would have made for greater efficiency. The stonework of the outer casing was dressed from the top down, the ramps and scaffolding dismantled and cleared as finishing work progressed back to ground level.

Above: Sculpture of the Fourth Dynasty king Khafre, who reigned c. 2558 BC–c. 2532 BC. Khafre came to the throne on the death of his half-brother, Djedefre. It was the latter who first added "Sa Re" (Son of Re) to the royal nomenclature, and Khafre continued this titulary connection with the Sun God.

Opposite: Painted limestone stela depicting the Fourth Dynasty princess Nefretiabet. Her panther-skin garb is that of a priestess, although this term merely referred to a temple worker and did not imply any degree of theological training. Most such workers were male but women from the upper strata of Egyptian society were also employed in temple duties which included cult offerings to the gods.

The Great Sphinx

The word "sphinx" automatically conjures up an image of the Great Sphinx of Giza, pictured left. In fact the Egyptians carved a large number of these mythical creatures, which were very different from the predatory female Sphinx of Greek legend, killer of men who failed to solve her riddle. To the Egyptians sphinxes were benign representations, actual or symbolic, of their king and the gods.

The Great Sphinx, which is almost 240ft long and 65ft at its highest point, stands near the valley temple of Khafre, in whose image it was almost certainly carved. The body is that of a lion, an animal linked with the Sun God Re as well as being an obvious symbol of royal power. The lion was also regarded as a protector of sacred places, and sphinxes were thus used extensively to guard the approaches to temple complexes. Not all sphinxes took this form. Some bore the head of a hawk or ram, symbols of Horus and Amun respectively.

Above: Dwarfism was not uncommon in Ancient Egypt. Far from leading to ostracization, those with stunted growth appear to have enjoyed favored status and often reached positions of authority. Pictured is Seneb, chief of the palace dwarfs, with his wife Senetites and children. Seneb was responsible for the royal wardrobe and was also priest of the funerary cults of the Fourth Dynasty kings Khufu and Dedefre.

Above: This life-size statue of the late Fourth–early Fifth Dynasty lector-priest Ka-aper, carved from sycamore, is regarded as one of the masterpieces of the Old Kingdom. It was discovered by the French Egyptologist Auguste Mariette, who excavated Ka-aper's mastaba tomb at Saqqara in the mid-nineteenth century. The figure reminded the excavating team of the headman of their village and they dubbed it "Sheikh el-Beled," which is Arabic for that title.

Opposite: One of a number of triad statues discovered in Menkaura's pyramid complex, which was excavated in 1908. On Menkaura's right is the goddess Hathor, daughter of Re and thus regarded as divine mother of the reigning king. Hathor was associated with many of life's pleasures, including music and sexual love. She was portrayed in several forms, one of which was the headdress comprising wig, cow horns, and sun disk seen here. On Menkaura's left is the personification of the seventeenth nome, or province, of Upper Egypt. The country was divided into forty-two nomes—twenty-two in Upper Egypt, twenty in Lower Egypt—each having its own symbol and governed by a nomarch.

Right: A Fifth Dynasty relief from Saqqara showing two women singing and playing the harp. The Egyptians had a range of wind, string, and percussion instruments, and music was ingrained in the culture. Nor was it just for festive occasions; work was done to a rhythmic accompaniment and music was also an integral part of religious ceremonies.

Below: A relief from the Old Kingdom depicting hunters in papyrus boats with captured birds and lotus blossoms. Papyrus grew in abundance round the Nile delta and was a symbol of Lower Egypt, while the lotus was associated with Upper Egypt. Both also featured prominently in the country's creation mythology.

Opposite: Alabaster panel decorated in sunken relief with an image of the Fifth Dynasty official Rawer, discovered in his tomb at Giza.

Above and opposite above: Sketches from the Fifth Dynasty unfinished chapel of Neferherptah depicting a bird-catching scene and a gardener cutting lettuce.

Opposite: Relief from the Saqqara tomb of the Fifth Dynasty vizier Ptahhotep. A hunter returns with caged birds while those previously caught have their wings broken. The vizier was Egypt's senior administrator, a factotum of the king overseeing the entire range of government activity. He reported directly to the king on fiscal, legal, and defense matters, and organized the labor force that was conscripted to work on state projects. The chief area where the vizier did not deputize for the king was in religious ceremonies. The ruler's sons were often appointed vizier during the Old Kingdom but this practice subsequently died out. From the Eighteenth Dynasty two viziers were appointed, to take responsibility for the affairs of Upper and Lower Egypt respectively. In the latter centuries of the Pharaonic era the power and status of the vizier appear to have diminished.

Right: King Neferikare's pyramid at Abusir, which was the main necropolis for Fifth Dynasty kings. The tomb complex of Neferikare, who reigned c. 2475 BC–c. 2455 BC, was meant to be larger than that of his predecessor, Sahure, but it was unfinished. However, it did yield a quantity of papyri which provided the best documentary evidence from the Old Kingdom relating to temple administration and the organization of funerary cults, including staffing arrangements and the offerings that were to be made. Neferikare's son, Niuserre, incorporated some of the unfinished construction work intended for his father into the design of his own pyramid complex.

Above: This head, carved in greywacke, is uninscribed but was found near the sun temple of Userkaf at Abusir and is thought to represent the king who founded the Fifth Dynasty. Userkaf's pyramid is at Saqqara, and his decision to build a separate sun temple at nearby Abusir set a precedent followed by several of his successors. Six such temples are known to have been built but only two, those associated with Userkaf and Niuserre, have been discovered thus far.

Opposite: Wooden statuette of a bearer from the tomb of Niankhpepi, a senior official to the Sixth Dynasty king Pepi I whose title was "Supervisor of Upper Egypt, Chancellor of the King of Lower Egypt." Niankhpepi's tomb was one of the most important to be discovered at Meir in Middle Egypt.

Left: One of three statues recovered from the Sixth Dynasty tomb of Merye-haishtef at Sedment in 1920 by a team led by Flinders Petrie. It shows Merye-haishtef as a striding youth, while other figures depict him as landowner and elder. The practice of placing in the tomb wooden statues of the deceased at different ages and in different poses is typical of the late Old Kingdom period.

Opposite above: Relief of a person sniffing a lotus blossom, from the mastaba tomb of Mereruka at Saqqara. Mereruka was vizier during the reign of Teti, the king who founded the Sixth Dynasty. He gained high office through marriage to the king's daughter, Princess Watetkhethor. His mastaba is the largest non-royal tomb of the Old Kingdom era, containing thirty-two chambers. These are decorated with numerous scenes depicting Mereruka and his wife going about their daily business, some of the best evidence of what life was like c. 2350 BC.

Opposite below: A relief from Mereruka's tomb showing metalworkers employed in the manufacture of jewelry. They use blowpipes on the forge to maintain its temperature. The tomb shows a variety of craftsmen at work, including masons, sculptors, and carpenters.

Below: Scene from the Sixth Dynasty mastaba tomb of Kagemni, who was vizier during the early part of Teti's reign. Animals feature prominently, with many images of hunting and fishing using nets and spears. Cattle were kept for their milk (as shown here), for meat, and as draft animals. Another scene from Kagemni's tomb shows a swineherd giving milk to a piglet. This is more unusual, since pigs were associated with Seth, the god of chaos. However, there is evidence of extensive pig-rearing in the later Pharaonic era.

Opposite above: A scene depicting an ox being slaughtered, from the tomb of Iti at Gebelein. This site, almost 20 miles south of Thebes, contains a number of tombs dating from the First Intermediate period, although others date back to the Predynastic era. The leg of an ox was sometimes used in the Opening of the Mouth ceremony (see page 144), possibly to pass on the beast's formidable strength to the deceased.

Opposite below: A painting from the tomb of Iti depicting a donkey transporting baskets of grain to the granary, where they are met by porters who carry the baskets up to the charge-hole.

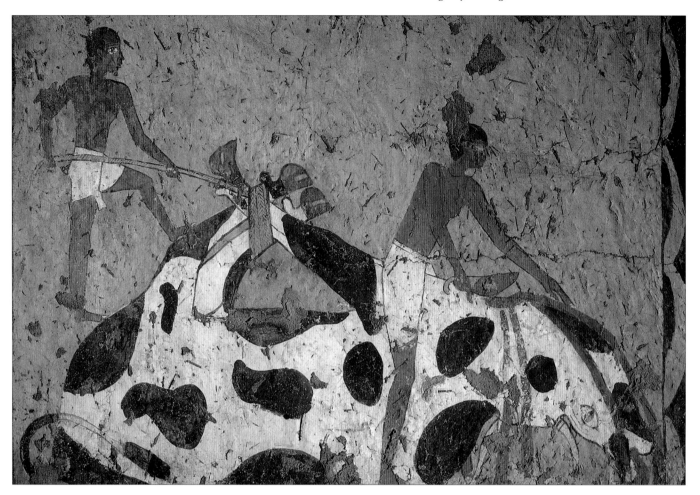

CHAPTER THREE

Prosperity and Power
c. 2181–1550 BC

Between the end of the Old Kingdom and beginning of the next great age there was a turbulent period lasting some 130 years. This is something of a twilight era but it is known that there was a multitude of brief reigns. There was undoubtedly political instability and a degree of fragmentation, disorder on a scale that was anathema to the Egyptians.

The Seventh and Eighth Dynasty kings continued to rule from the old capital, Memphis, and Saqqara remained the most important royal necropolis. However, their power base was soon under threat from powerful forces in Upper Egypt. The Ninth Dynasty was probably founded by Khety c. 2160 BC. Khety was a nomarch who apparently seized the throne and established a seat of power at Herakleopolis. During the Tenth Dynasty there was political friction between Herakleopolis and Thebes. The latter had been a small provincial center during the Old Kingdom, but after an official named Mentuhotep established strong dynastic control over the town it looked to challenge the authority of Herakleopolis. For a time these centers vied for the political ascendancy and for the allegiance of other Egyptian provinces. The Herakleopolitan Tenth Dynasty and Theban Eleventh Dynasty thus ran concurrently for some time. Thebes eventually won out after the fifth king of that lineage, Mentuhotep II, wrested control of the entire land. It is uncertain whether this was achieved by force or negotiation, but the hegemony

of Thebes over its rival, c. 2055 BC, saw Egypt return to political cohesion. Mentuhotep II became the first king of the Middle Kingdom, a new golden era which would last for 400 years.

Deir el-Bahri

Mentuhotep II reigned for some fifty years, with the capital now at Thebes. It was a period of political and economic consolidation which included stamping out internal resistance, waging a number of military campaigns against neighboring lands, and re-establishing important trading links. The building of monuments on a grand scale resumed, and art and literature flourished.

For his funerary complex Mentuhotep II chose Deir el-Bahri on the west bank of the Nile opposite Luxor. The mortuary temple was of an unusual terraced design. It faced east, suggesting that the cult of the Sun God was still to the fore, and also incorporated a structure thought to symbolize the primeval mound of the creation myth. The complex accommodated six of Mentuhotep's queens, whose magnificent limestone sarcophagi were later discovered. Mentuhotep's burial chamber did not survive to the modern era intact but a sandstone statue was discovered in the early twentieth century. The skin was painted black, one of the characteristic representations of Osiris, god of the Underworld and resurrection.

Opposite: Mummiform inner coffin of Sepi, a Twelfth Dynasty general. It bears the nemes headcloth and false beard, both associated with kingship, suggesting that Sepi was an important military leader.

Amenemhat

Little is known of the reigns of the next two Eleventh Dynasty kings, Mentuhotep III and Mentuhotep IV. They inherited a peaceful and prosperous country, but violence and disorder marked the end of the latter's reign and the establishment of a new royal line. Mentuhotep IV's vizier, Amenemhat, appears to have seized the throne in a bloody coup. Certainly Amenemhat I founded the Twelfth Dynasty c. 1985 BC and it is widely assumed that the two men are one and the same. Amenemhat moved quickly to legitimize his accession and impose his will. He may have been responsible for a document purporting to date from the Fourth Dynasty and "foretelling" the coming of a man of non-royal birth who would bring order to a troubled country. The capital was again relocated, from Thebes to Itjtawy, south of Memphis. This translates as "Seizer of the Two Lands," an overt indication of Amenemhat's dubious claim to the throne.

Having gained power, Amenemhat sought to insure that he didn't suffer the same fate as his predecessor. Regional governors were either placemen or were granted privileges and concessions aimed to forestall discontent. He is also thought to have introduced the practice of co-regency to aid the smooth transition between the deceased king and the new incumbent. Thus Amenemhat's son and successor, Senusret I, became joint ruler in the latter years of his reign, a decision which seems to have been vindicated as there is documentary evidence indicating that the father was assassinated.

Amun-Re

In this period an important theological shift occurred. Amun became pre-eminent among the Egyptian pantheon at the behest of the Twelfth Dynasty kings. Indeed Amenemhat's very name translates as "Amun is at the head." Amun's position as "King of the Gods" was further reinforced after he was later merged with the Sun God Re to form Amun-Re. Amun's cult center was Thebes, and the temple dedicated to him at Karnak is one of the best surviving complexes of the era. However, in Egypt as a whole—rather than just the royal court—Osiris was elevated to the role of the most important deity. Egyptians made considerable effort to pay homage to the god of death and resurrection. There were pilgrimages to Abydos, Osiris's cult center, and some chose to be buried there, or for the mummy to be taken there temporarily before interment elsewhere. Boat models featured in funerary equipment, allowing the journey to Abydos to be made post mortem.

Amenemhat chose el-Lisht, south of Dahshur, for the new royal necropolis. Both his funerary complex

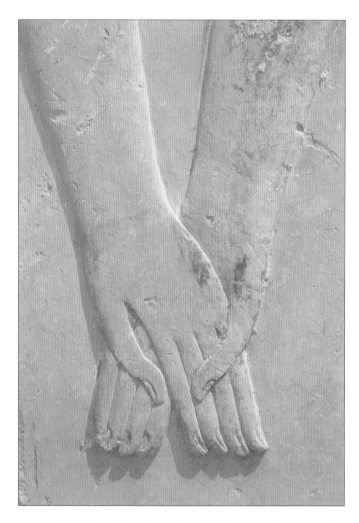

Above: Relief from the White Chapel of the Twelfth Dynasty king Senusret I, built to celebrate the sed *festival, the royal jubilee during which rituals of renewal and regeneration were performed. This festival was meant to be conducted after 30 years of unbroken rule, although there is evidence that it took place during the reigns of kings who were on the throne for a much shorter time.*

and that of his son Senusret I saw a return to pyramid construction, although at around 60m these were less than half the size of Khufu's Great Pyramid at Giza.

The Twelfth Dynasty

Senusret I successfully continued to assert territorial control over Nubia, an expansionist policy begun by his father. Amenemhat II, Senusret's son who came to power c. 1922 BC, concentrated on establishing commercial links rather than conquest. In 1936 a number of silver vessels were discovered at a temple site at Tod. These were inscribed with Amenemhat's name and were of western Asian or Mediterranean origin. Whether these were gifts, tribute, or traded goods, they provide clear evidence of commercial links with the Near East. This set the pattern for the remainder of the Twelfth Dynasty, Egypt enjoying economic and military strength and considerable stability.

Senusret III

Three rulers, Amenemhat II, Senusret III, and Amenemhat III, chose to site their funerary complexes at Dahshur, though the last of these abandoned the project and built a second pyramid at Hawara in the Faiyum region. This complex includes a mortuary temple containing 3000 interconnecting rooms, known as the Labyrinth. It was not only the largest building of its kind but is said to be bigger than all the other temples combined. The pyramids of this time were constructed more cheaply than their solid stone Old Kingdom counterparts. That of Amenemhat III subsequently had its limestone casing removed or stolen to reveal a mudbrick core which eventually fell victim to erosion.

The reign of the Twelfth Dynasty's fifth king, Senusret

III (c. 1874 BC–c. 1855 BC), was a high-water mark. He oversaw the construction of a number of fortresses to extend Egypt's dominion over Nubia still farther; he ordered channels to be dug which considerably improved communications via the Nile; and he revised the administrative system to take direct control of state affairs through his viziers, rather than via the nomarchs. This was a clear attempt to emasculate the provincial governors and reduce the chance of any of them challenging the royal prerogative.

Senusret III's legacy, enjoyed by the last three Twelfth Dynasty rulers, was a country that was the richest, most

Below: Twelfth Dynasty boat model. From the Middle Kingdom boats were placed within tombs to allow the deceased to travel to Abydos, the cult center of Osiris. According to myth, Osiris's body, dismembered by his brother Seth, was magically restored to life, making him the chief god associated with resurrection. Abydos remained an important religious site through to the period of Roman control, some 2000 years later.

Left: Model servant girl carrying loaves and meat. During the Old Kingdom shabti *servants were usually individual figures; by the Middle Kingdom models of entire groups of workers, engaged in baking, brewing, or other aspects of food production, were commonplace in tombs. By the New Kingdom (c. 1550 BC–c. 1069 BC) the number of* shabti *figures could be as high as 365, one for every day of the year. The word probably derives from "ushabti," meaning "answerer," since the figure was expected to respond to the call to toil. The* shabti's *duties are covered in Chapter six of the Book of the Dead.*

Opposite: A goldfish amulet, worn by young women to protect against drowning in the Nile. Egyptians made no clear distinction between science and magic. Hundreds of different amulets have been found, all offering protection on the journey to the afterlife. There were specific instructions, described in the Book of the Dead, relating to how and where these amulets should be brought into contact with the deceased's body.

powerful and culturally advanced on earth. The dynasty came to an end with the short reign of the first attested female pharaoh, Sobekneferu, who may have been the sister and wife of her predecessor, Amenemhat IV.

The Thirteenth Dynasty

The Thirteenth Dynasty, which began c. 1795 BC and lasted some 150 years, was characterized by numerous short reigns. Initially the systems and practices adopted by Senusret III to maintain Egypt's position of strength were maintained. The brief regnal periods—the average was less than three years—meant that there were no spectacular funerary monuments. The succession of around seventy rulers seems to have been more by usurpation than bloodline, and decline set in. One of the first casualties was the powerful border defenses that had been established in the previous dynasty. The grip over Nubia was relaxed, while in the north there were incursions by Asiatics—peoples from modern-day Palestine and its environs—notably at Tell el-Daba in the delta region.

The Fourteenth Dynasty

During the last century of the Middle Kingdom, c. 1750 BC–c. 1650 BC, Egypt was in a state of flux. A political schism occurred when a breakaway faction in the eastern delta region established a new royal line—the Fourteenth Dynasty—which seems to have run in parallel with the Thirteenth. This secessionist line was short-lived as piecemeal incursion from the north turned into full-scale invasion. At around this time the mainstream royal line of the Thirteenth Dynasty removed from Itjtawy to Thebes. For a time the three separate power blocs—two rival internal dynasties and the Asiatic invaders—probably operated concurrently. When the Fourteenth Dynasty rulers finally lost their power base in the delta region, it left two opposing political forces. At first there was an accommodation between the invaders who controlled Lower Egypt and the established Egyptian line based at Thebes. It was only a matter of time, however, before the Egyptians came into direct conflict with the people dubbed Hyksos—"rulers of foreign lands."

Opposite: In this wood and plaster sculpture, c. 2040 BC, a cook fans the fire in preparation for roasting the duck he holds in his left hand. The use of models dates back to the First Dynasty but by the Middle Kingdom they were far more elaborate. Models were merely an extension of two-dimensional images; both were believed able to fulfil the role they illustrated. Ancient Egyptians thought that painted images could carry out a symbolic function, while models would be magically reconstituted to full size and animated to service their master's needs in the afterlife.

Above: A wooden model of a woman grinding grain. The placing of an offering table at the funerary site was important for all strata of society throughout the Pharaonic period. It was here that priests or relatives brought offerings to sustain the deceased's ka. During the Middle Kingdom it became common practice for the tombs of the poorer classes to include pottery models of their homes. Food was placed in the courtyard of these soul houses, which were effectively a more elaborate version of the simple offering table. They thus combined the twin ideas of the need to feed the soul after death and the fact that the tomb was the deceased's spiritual home.

Opposite: Servant girl bearing offerings for Meketre, an Eleventh Dynasty nobleman. His was one of the most important private tombs to be discovered at Deir el-Bahri, containing a number of beautifully crafted funerary models. Such figures were engaged in various types of food production or activities such as weaving and carpentry.

Above: Wooden model scene from the tomb of Meketre depicting the nobleman inspecting and counting his cattle herd.

Right: Model sycamore tree from Meketre's tomb. As well as food, possessions, and servants, models were also included to provide entertainment and relaxation. Musicians and dwarfs, pet animals, and concubine figures came into this category.

Above: Wooden model of carpenters at work, found in the tomb of Meketre at Deir el-Bahri.

Right: Middle Kingdom wooden sculpture of an emaciated figure holding a bowl. Even the poorest had high expectations of the afterlife. While the kings took their place among the gods and the wealthy enjoyed the luxuries with which they were buried—either real or images thereof—the poor anticipated working the land in Osiris's kingdom. Although this involved strenuous toil the Underworld was a land of plenty where contentment was assured.

Opposite above: This shabti *figure, complete with model coffin, is one of the earliest extant examples of its kind. It was discovered in the tomb of a Thirteenth Dynasty prince, Wahneferhotep.*

The Golden Age of Literature

Throughout the Old Kingdom Egyptian literature consisted mainly of business accounts, private letters, and increasingly detailed funerary inscriptions, culminating in the Pyramid Texts. The Middle Kingdom is regarded as the golden age of this art form. Instructive texts and stories appeared for the first time, although these may have been based on an oral tradition. Both had a didactic element. The instructive texts offered maxims by which the model Egyptian could lead a successful and righteous life. One of the most celebrated is that given by Amenemhat I to his son, Senusret, describing how his benign rule was repaid with disloyalty and an assassination conspiracy before he was able to elevate his son to coregent. As Senusret I did indeed reign jointly with his father, the text seems to be a judicious warning rather than a representation of actual events.

Of the fictional narratives which appeared during this period the Tale of Sinuhe is regarded as a masterpiece. The courtier of the title is living in exile, having fled Egypt on the death of Amenemhat I. Although he has forged a successful new life he craves to return to the land of his birth. Senusret I answers his plea and Sinuhe returns home to a triumphant reconciliation at court. The tale ends with his glorious death and spectacular burial.

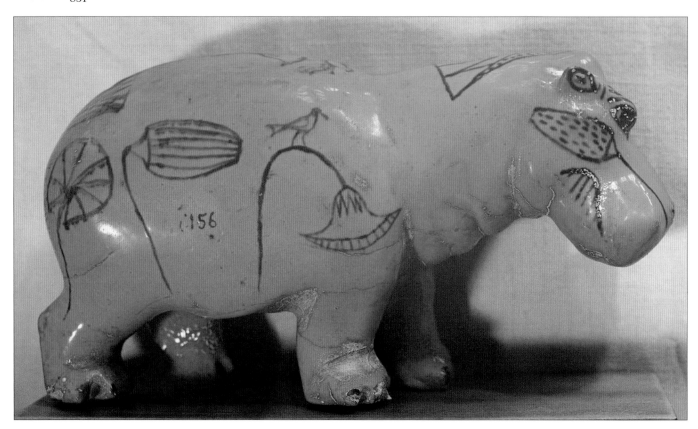

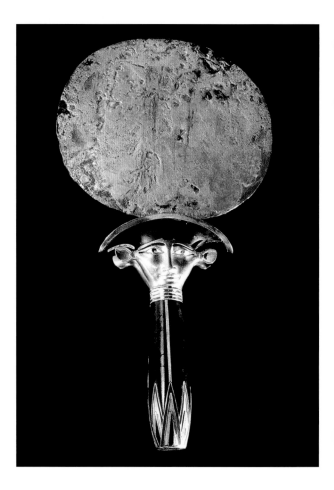

Above: Middle Kingdom statuette of a hippopotamus, made from blue faience and decorated with images of papyrus and other water plants. The male hippopotamus, along with the crocodile, was deemed a threat to both people and crops and thus a force for evil. Hippopotamus hunts date from the Predynastic era. Kings were often involved, and such hunts assumed ritual significance: the delivery of the coup de grace was seen as a symbolic representation of Horus's slaying of Seth, and thus a victory of good over evil. The female of the species, by contrast, was a benign figure. Tawaret, the goddess associated with the protection of women in childbirth, was portrayed as a hippopotamus, in which form she often appeared in bed designs and on amulets. During the Middle Kingdom hippopotami figurines, often decorated with images of vegetation, were regularly included in funerary goods, probably for their association with strength and regeneration.

Opposite: This exquisite silver mirror has an obsidian papyrus-shaped handle depicting the head of Hathor, the bovine goddess associated with sexual love. It belonged to Princess Sithathoriunet, daughter of the Middle Kingdom pharaoh Senusret II, whose tomb was unearthed by Flinders Petrie in 1914. The fact that the princess's name also incorporated that of Hathor would have guaranteed her youthful beauty both in the mortal world and beyond.

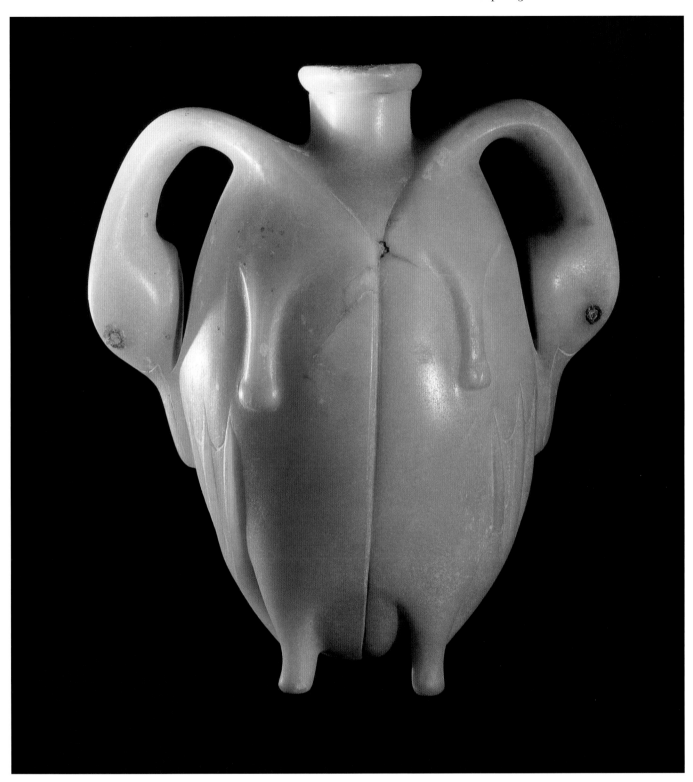

Above: Blue marble ointment jar in the shape of two ducks trussed in readiness for sacrifice. Medicine was a combination of prescriptions—based on knowledge of the human body— ritual and magic. A number of papyri describing remedies for various conditions and ailments have survived. Doctors were skilled at setting broken bones, cauterizing wounds, and applying sutures of string using needles made from bone.

Honey was used as a disinfectant, while onion juice was favored for its antibiotic properties. The excrement of a number of different creatures featured in remedies, the belief being that waste products within the body were a common cause of complaint and had to be treated on a like-for-like basis. The use of amulets, charms, and spells was seen as an integral part of the healing process.

Left: Human-faced heart scarab, the most important of the amulets used during burial rituals. In the mummification process such scarabs were placed within the bandaging over the deceased's heart, and bore an inscription exhorting that organ not to reveal any misdeeds when it was weighed during the judgement ceremony before Osiris.

Below: Unguent chest containing alabaster jars and a mirror. The ivory front panel shows the owner, a servant of the king in the royal household, offering ointment jars to the deified statue of his master.

Above: Container for perfumed oil in the shape of a cat. This creature was much admired for its ability to fight snakes, although it may not have been until the New Kingdom that cats were kept as pets. The cat was a symbol of the goddess Bastet, whose name derives from "bas," meaning ointment jar. She was thus associated with efficaciousness and healing. In the Later Dynastic period Bastet was often depicted with kittens, reflecting a protective quality. Cats were among those animals who were accorded burial rituals, including mummification. Many cat graves have been found found at Bubastis, Bastet's cult center in the delta.

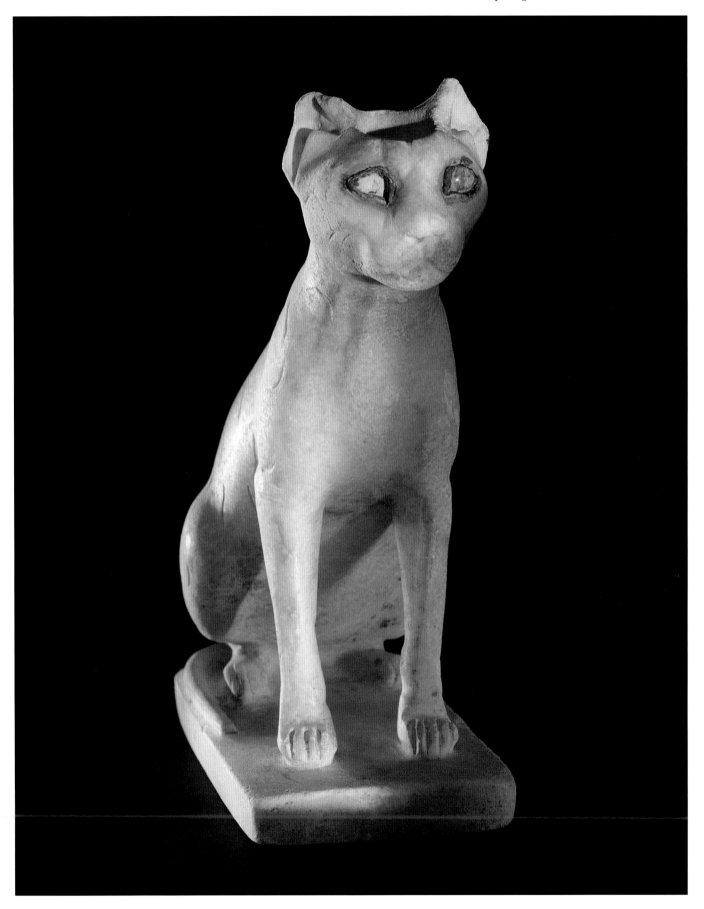

Above: Fragment of a painted relief from the south wall of the funerary temple of Mentuhotep II, depicting a jackal raiding a bird's nest. The jackal was a common scavenger. It is thought that Anubis, god of embalming and mummification, was portrayed with a jackal's head to stave off the threat these creatures posed to corpses.

Right: Detail of a Middle Kingdom king-list depicting a bee, symbol of the north of Egypt. King-lists were regularly found in royal mortuary temples as the deceased ruler claimed his place in the royal lineage. Offerings were made to previous kings as well as the recently deceased ruler.

Opposite: Fragment of the temple wall of Mentuhotep II.

Above: Relief from the White Chapel of Senusret I at Karnak, which was built to celebrate the sed festival. The king (right) pays homage to Min, god of fertility. Min is depicted in typical pose, with erect phallus, right hand raised in readiness to strike, and twin-plumed headdress. As the sed festival was concerned with renewal and regeneration Min featured prominently, reaffirming the king's potency.

Opposite: Middle Kingdom statue thought to depict Amenemhat III, sixth king of the Twelfth Dynasty. Amenemhat presided over a country that was economically and militarily strong, the legacy of his predecessor Senusret III. He built two pyramids, one at Dahshur —which was uninscribed and may have been a cenotaph—the other at Hawara in the Faiyum region, his probable burial site.

Opposite: Middle Kingdom bronze bust, thought to be of Amenemhat IV, the last male ruler of the Twelfth Dynasty. His rule and that of his successor, Queen Sobekneferu, saw the beginning of a new period of decline. Political instability followed, with numerous brief reigns of competing dynasties. As well as internal conflict, Egypt faced the problem of infiltration from beyond its shores as outsiders sought to capitalize on the country's weakness.

Right: Outer coffin of the Middle Kingdom general, Sepi. At this time rectangular coffins were oriented in a north–south plane with the body placed on its left side, facing east. Eyes were painted on the coffin's eastern face to afford a view of the rising sun and images of sustenance. Inscriptions of spells on the coffin insured safe passage to the afterlife. Coffin Texts were a development of the Old Kingdom Pyramid Texts and were no longer the exclusive preserve of royalty. A false door through which the spirit could pass was also incorporated into the coffin design.

CHAPTER FOUR

The New Kingdom
c. 1550–1069 BC

The founding of the Eighteenth Dynasty, c.1550 BC, ushered in a 500-year period regarded as the last great age of the Pharaonic era. The New Kingdom, as it is called, saw the establishment of a new royal necropolis, the famous Valley of the Kings, where Howard Carter unearthed the tomb of Tutankhamun in 1922. There was also a seismic shift in the theological orthodoxy before the period ended in economic hardship, social unrest, and imperial decline.

The Hyksos

From 1650 BC there was a century in which the Egyptians struggled to reclaim their land from the northeastern invader known as the Hyksos. It is said that the latter, led by King Tutimaios, conquered Egypt without a struggle and instituted a vicious regime in which the indigenous population was cruelly subjugated. One explanation for the apparent ease with which the Hyksos gained control is that Asiatic peoples had been migrating to Egypt over a period of time and resistance to invasion was thus diluted. A new capital was established at Avaris in the delta region—possibly modern-day Tell el-Daba—and Salitis was promoted from the ranks to become the first Hyksos ruler of Egypt.

However, other sources maintain that the invaders were much more accommodating, seeking to rule by consent rather than impose their iron will.

It is suggested that in fact the Hyksos readily adopted the mores of Egyptian society. Seth was elevated to the position of pre-eminent deity, but this was probably simply to do with the fact that he was identified with a member of the Hyskos pantheon, rather than a deliberate attempt to subvert the theological status quo by revering a god the Egyptians associated with evil. It is possible that the uncharitable view of the Hyksos became common currency because it made their ultimate expulsion from the country a more glorious triumph.

The period of Hyksos rule was one of innovation: there were advances in craft and construction skills; new weaponry, including bronze swords and daggers, was introduced; the lyre and lute arrived to join Egypt's indigenous stringed instrument, the harp; and the horse and chariot were seen in the country for the first time.

Notwithstanding these benefits, relations worsened between the Hyksos and the line of Egyptian princes who were satellite rulers of Thebes. The Hyksos were themselves divided, two dynasties running concurrently in Lower Egypt. Neither line made great inroads southwards, leaving Thebes with a degree of autonomy which eventually led to a planned uprising. The clash began under the Theban ruler Seqenenre, whose skull was split by a blow from an axe, almost certainly a battle wound. His successor, Kamose, waged a successful military campaign and the

Opposite: Wall painting from the Eighteenth Dynasty tomb of Pere, depicting the tomb owner and his wife before an altar laden with offerings. Flowers featured prominently in the festive scenes on the walls of non-royal tombs during this period. They *appeared both in garland form as decorative adornment, and also being held close to the nose. The Egyptians' love of scented flowers and all pleasurable smells can be inferred from the fact that the nose was the hieroglyph for the verb "to enjoy."*

Above: The village of Deir el-Medina, situated on Thebes' west bank, was built in the Eighteenth Dynasty to house the workers who constructed the Valley of the Kings. It declined at the end of the Twentieth Dynasty when Tanis became the site of the new royal necropolis.

overthrow of the Hyksos was completed by the next in the Theban line, Amosis. Having driven out the enemy, he founded the Eighteenth Dynasty as Amosis I. With his rule the Second Intermediate period was brought to an end and the New Kingdom was launched, a period widely regarded as the greatest of the Pharaonic era.

Tuthmosis

The experience of the Hyksos invasion made Amosis I and his immediate successors more bellicose. A professional army was formed for the first time as Egypt not only sought to insure her borders would not again be breached, but also to extend her territory by conquest. There were successful forays south into Nubia and as far north as the Euphrates. By the reign of the third Eighteenth Dynasty king,

Above: Sketch of an acrobatic dancer, painted on a shard of limestone known as ostracon. Such fragments were commonly used for preliminary artwork as it was a cheaper alternative to papyrus.

Tuthmosis I, Egypt's sphere of influence stretched farther than ever before. Tuthmosis was also the first ruler to choose the remote cliffs on the west bank of the Nile at Thebes for his burial site. This set a precedent for successive New Kingdom pharaohs; thus three dynasties over a 500-year period were entombed in what has come to be known as the Valley of the Kings. The main reason for choosing deep rock-cut tombs over pyramids seems to have been a deterrent to grave-robbers. If so it was a forlorn hope, for every tomb save that of Tutankhamun was plundered in antiquity.

As well as being home to the royal necropolis, Thebes was the center of political power and the country's most important religious site. Amun, a local deity since the Eleventh Dynasty, was now Amun-Re, the omnipotent creator god. Eighteenth Dynasty pharaohs added to and embellished the temple complex dedicated to Amun at Karnak, only too willing to lavish resources on the god associated with restoring Egypt's proud independence. This eventually had disastrous consequences as the priesthood at Karnak began to wield economic and political power which posed a direct threat to the throne.

One area where this burgeoning influence was exercised was in the royal succession. On the death of

Tuthmosis I the throne passed to his son. Tuthmosis II married his half-sister, Hatshepsut, who bore him a daughter. The king's nominated heir was his only son— also called Tuthmosis—whose mother was one of the royal concubines. Tuthmosis II died young, and with his nominated successor still a child, Hatshepsut acted as regent. With the backing of the priests of Amun the ambitious Hatshepsut proclaimed herself pharaoh, relegating Tuthmosis III to a twenty-year period in which he was nominally coregent but effectively emasculated. Hatshepsut consolidated her position by claiming divine lineage, promoting the idea that Amun had impregnated her mother. Her claim to be the "female Horus" was unique; this was an alien concept to the Ancient Egyptians and the iconography of her reign presents her in masculine form.

Hatshepsut's reign seems to have been largely peaceful and successful, a period in which trade flourished. However, when Tuthmosis III finally came to power—either by seizing the throne or on Hatshepsut's death—he went to some lengths to obliterate his predecessor from the historical record. This does not seem to have been done out of spite or revenge, but simply to remove from king-lists someone who had no right to appear therein.

The Aten and Monotheism

Tuthmosis III proved to be an outstanding military leader, waging a number of successful campaigns in the Near East. These included the capture of Megiddo, where a coalition of rebel forces who had tried to regain their independence from Egypt was crushed after a seven-month siege. For a time it seems the country enjoyed its power and wealth unchallenged since the need to take military action subsided. However, this was merely the calm before an internal storm which had dramatic consequences for the latter stages of the Eighteenth Dynasty. It was both a political and theological issue. At its heart was the growing interest in the cult of the Aten. Like Re, the Aten was a solar deity who, prior to the New Kingdom, had had minor status in the Egyptian pantheon. By the time Amenhotep III acceded to the throne, c. 1390 BC, the Aten had begun to challenge the established deific order, and this was inevitably tantamount to a challenge on the Karnak priesthood.

The Aten was often depicted as a solar disk with rays emanating therefrom. These took the form of outstretched hands, some holding the *ankh*, the sign of life associated with royal and divine power. Amenhotep III had already defied tradition by choosing Tiy as his Great Royal Wife, the title held by the king's senior consort. As a non-royal Tiy was unlikely to have been favored by the priesthood, and Amenhotep may have

regarded marriage to her as a means of imposing his will. The king's endorsement of the cult of the Aten raised the stakes considerably, although it was during the reign of his successor—his son Amenhotep IV—that the power of the throne over the senior priests asserted itself most dramatically. Under the latter's rule monotheism replaced pantheism, a state of affairs Egypt had never known. All other gods, including Amun-Re, were proscribed. As Amenhotep's very name meant "Amun is content," he changed it to Akhenaten— "Glorious is the Aten." The power of the priesthood was curtailed virtually at a stroke and a number of temples dedicated to the new sole creator god were built.

Akhenaten

Having begun his reign at Thebes, Akhenaten now sought a new capital, a center for secular power and religious worship untainted by the past. The site chosen was Akhetaten—"Horizon of the Aten"—some 300km north of Thebes, near modern-day el-Amarna. It was virgin territory, reinforcing the fact that this represented a break with Egyptian tradition, and hordes of workers were drafted in to construct a city which may have accommodated up to 50,000 people. The planning included a site for a new royal necropolis. Akhetaten occupied a site on the east bank of the Nile, and the next kings were to be buried in a

Left: Detail of a wall painting from the Theban tomb of Userhet, showing gifts of food provided by Hathor, in her aspect as tree goddess.

Opposite: Eighteenth Dynasty relief of a Nubian slave, almost certainly a prisoner of war. Slavery was rare through the Dynastic period. The peasant class was tied to the land, working for crown, temple, or nobles' estates, but this was more akin to serfdom than slavery. All strata of society had legal rights. All served the pharaoh, the embodiment of the state, who in return insured that Egypt remained a harmonious and bountiful land.

Overleaf: Bust of the Nineteenth Dynasty pharaoh Merenptah, from his mortuary temple at Thebes. He was the thirteenth son of Rameses II, who reigned for sixty-seven years and outlived many of his children.

mountainous area on the same side of the river. This meant that the symbolic east–west crossing of the Nile would not take place, another major departure from Egyptian tradition.

Akhenaten's singlemindedness came at a cost. He seems to have largely neglected his role as imperial overlord, and the establishment of a new city, together with the disestablishment of the priesthood, had a damaging effect on the economy. It was a period of great artistic achievement, but the royal court had become insular and inward-looking. Akhetaten was so remote from the Egyptian people—both literally and metaphorically—that the king's popularity declined considerably.

Akhenaten reigned for some eighteen years, during which time his famed chief wife, the beautiful Nefertiti, bore him six daughters. The king married two of his offspring in an attempt to produce a male heir who would take the revolutionary regime forward. This too failed and the throne passed to the shadowy figure of Smenkhkare. He may have been a son of Amenhotep III, the progeny of Akhenaten and another wife, or even son-in-law to the king. Smenkhkare's reign lasted a matter of months and on his death the throne passed to his younger brother, Tutankhaten. The nine-year-old boy-king was easy prey for the senior court advisors, who were now having misgivings about the entire cultural shift of the past generation. The experiment quickly unraveled. After only about thirty years in existence Akhetaten was abandoned in favor of a return to Thebes. Tutankhaten and his wife Ankhesenpaaten—Akhenaten's third daughter and one of those he also married—both renounced the "aten" suffix to their names, replacing it with "amun." It was now Akhenaten's turn to have his name and works excised from the records, and Egypt's brief flirtation with monotheism came to an end.

Tutankhamun

Tutankhamun died, possibly murdered, while still in his teens and was buried in the Valley of the Kings. Save for the part he played in undoing the heresies of the Akhenaten era he remained a largely unknown figure until Howard Carter's famous discovery of his magnificent tomb in 1922.

Tutankhamun left no natural heir, giving rise to another succession problem. The royal widow invited the King of the Hittites—a traditional enemy—to send one of his sons to marry her and claim the throne. A prince was duly dispatched but he was murdered en route. It is likely that the assassin was acting for Ay and Horemheb, two of Tutankhamun's senior advisors who had risen to prominence during Akhenaten's reign and latterly become prime movers in the counter-revolution. Certainly Ay took the opportunity to marry Tutankhamun's widow, Ankhesenamun. After his four-year rule Horemheb, a former military commander, acceded to the throne. Horemheb's wife, Mutnefert, may have been Nefertiti's sister, but irrespective of the strength of his claim, the new king spent the next twenty-seven years expunging all traces of what is now called the Amarna period and restoring Egypt to her former glory.

The Nineteenth Dynasty

With Horemheb's death the Eighteenth Dynasty came to an end. The nominated successor was Rameses, a former army comrade of the king who had risen to the rank of

vizier. The founder of the Nineteenth Dynasty died after barely a year in office, succeeded by his son, Seti I. The new ruler waged several successful military campaigns, notably against the Hittites and Libyans, and was also responsible for some spectacular monuments. One such was his own mortuary temple at Abydos, and he also consolidated Amun's return to pre-eminence with the Great Hypostyle Hall at Karnak. This has a dense forest of huge columns adorned with papyrus motifs to symbolize the reedbank and watery chaos from which life sprang.

Seti's son, Rameses II, reigned for sixty-six years. He completed the Great Hypostyle Hall and farther extended the Karnak complex. Other impressive construction projects included his mortuary temple at Thebes, the Ramasseum, and the two temples at Abu Simbel in Nubia. The latter has a façade of four 20m-high statues of the seated king. Beneath his feet are the Nine Bows. These represented Egypt's traditional enemies, including Nubians, Libyans, and Asiatics, who were often depicted being crushed underfoot, emphasizing Egypt's supremacy. The larger of the temples is orientated such that twice a year, on February 22 and October 22, the first rays at dawn illuminate the statues of the gods in the innermost chamber.

Rameses II also relocated the seat of government from Thebes to the harbor town of Qantir in the eastern delta, which remained Egypt's capital for the remainder of the New Kingdom.

There was yet another protracted conflict with the Hittites. Records describe the king's leadership and valor, but in fact the war was only brought to an end by negotiation. As relations thawed, Rameses tried to forestall further hostilities by adding two Hittite princesses to his concubines.

Rameses II is believed to have fathered over 100 children, but his longevity meant that it was his thirteenth son, Merenptah, who succeeded him. The Nineteenth Dynasty's fourth king was probably nearing sixty when he came to the throne. The most noteworthy event of his ten-year reign was the successful repulse of an attempted invasion by a coalition of Libyans and disparate migrants from the eastern Mediterranean known as the Sea Peoples. The invaders were not aiming to conquer; they were displaced peoples seeking to put down roots, no doubt drawn to Egypt's natural riches. That benign motive didn't prevent Merenptah from meting out ruthless treatment, which included taking 6000 lives. This great victory was recorded for posterity on the walls of the Temple of Amun.

The last four Nineteenth Dynasty rulers occupied the throne for only some seventeen years in total. It was a period of confusion and intrigue. Merenptah's son and designated successor, Seti II, was temporarily prevented from gaining the throne by the usurper Amenmessu, a son of one of Rameses II's daughters. The dynasty ended with the brief reign of Queen Tausret, wife of Seti II.

The Twentieth Dynasty

The Twentieth Dynasty was established by Sethnakhte, of whom little is known. His son, Rameses III, who reigned for over thirty years, is regarded as the last great pharaoh. He made his mark on the battlefield early on, given the opportunity to cover himself in glory by yet another attack from the Sea Peoples. The king recorded his great victory on the walls of his mortuary temple at Medinet Habu on Thebes' west bank.

The last twenty years of Rameses III's reign were peaceful and he oversaw some impressive building projects, including an addition to the Karnak complex and his own tomb in the Valley of the Kings. Toward the end of Rameses' reign the economy faltered and there was discontent at Deir el-Medina among palace workers, who went on strike over food rations. There was an attempted coup involving one of the royal wives, and although Rameses survived to see the plotters brought to justice he may have fallen victim to another attempt on his life.

The remaining eight kings of the Twentieth Dynasty all took Rameses' name, ruling for less than a century between them. All were weak rulers, and a malaise set in. It was a period blighted by maladministration, economic decline, poor harvests, and a dissatisfied workforce. A smallpox epidemic added to the hardship and a spate of tomb robberies occurred, possibly indicating the desperation of the perpetrators. Nor were matters helped by the fact that the kings ruled from the delta, a long way from the traditional seat of power at Thebes.

Society had become polarized. Some enjoyed great wealth and a lavish lifestyle, others feathered their nests through corrupt practices, while for many it was a time of poverty and deprivation. By c. 1099 BC, when the last king of the dynasty, Rameses XI, ascended the throne, he was ruler in name only. There ensued a power struggle between Upper and Lower Egypt reminiscent of the period before Narmer united the country 2000 years earlier. Herihor, high priest of Amun at Thebes, exercised control over Upper Egypt and Nubia, while an official named Smendes ruled over the delta region from Tanis. There are reliefs showing Herihor wearing the Double Crown, and other sources accord him royal status. However, it was Smendes who prevailed to become the founding ruler of the Twenty-first Dynasty. The beginning of a new chapter in Egypt's history marked the end of a great imperial power. Nubia asserted its independence in the south, while territories held in the Near East were lost.

Above: The gateway to the Temple of Luxor, flanked by seated statues of Rameses II. It lies a short distance south of the vast temple complex at Karnak, the two sites linked by an avenue of sphinxes.

This was Egypt's most sacred religious site. Both temples were primarily dedicated to Amun, who became Egypt's principal deity during the Twelfth Dynasty.

Egyptian Temples

The Egyptians constructed two main types of temple, reflecting the dual focus of religious worship: the gods and the pharaoh, the latter having divine status and taking his place in the pantheon post mortem. Cult temples were built to honor the many deities, while rituals dedicated to the deceased god-kings were conducted in mortuary temples.

Cult temples developed in both form and function from the creation myth: belief in a creator god who brought forth land and life from watery chaos. All temple sites symbolized the primeval mound, and were built with a gradient rising toward the inner shrine to represent the island of creation. Here a cult statue of the god would reside, believed to be a repository for the deity's *ka* and in need of daily sustenance. These rituals could only be conducted by the king himself or delegated priests. Temples were thus not places of congregational worship; rather, the

rituals were conducted to maintain an established theological order and perpetuate a specific world view, known to the Egyptians as *maat*. Only during certain festivals, when the cult statues were taken on ceremonial journeys, were the masses able to participate in celebratory worship rituals.

Mortuary temples were something of a misnomer, since work on them was usually begun soon after the new pharaoh acceded to the throne and rituals could be conducted there prior to the king's death. Their function was twofold: to secure the deceased king's passage as he took his place among the gods, and thereafter for ritual offerings to preserve his name in perpetuity. As in the cult temples, a *ka* statue

of the king was provided with daily sustenance.

The royal—and thus divine—lineage was important to the pharaohs, who legitimized their own reign by seeking the approval of both the gods and their predecessors. However, the current incumbent naturally took precedence over former rulers, and older mortuary temples often fell into disrepair as resources were reallocated.

During the Old Kingdom mortuary temples were usually constructed on the east side of the king's pyramid. New Kingdom pharaohs entombed in the Valley of the Kings had their mortuary temples built some distance away, though the spiritual connection was maintained.

Above: Aerial view of the Temple of Amun, with the Temple of Montu and the modern village of Karnak to the right. Amun and Montu were both Theban tutelary deities. Montu, the falcon-headed god of war, was prominent during the Eleventh Dynasty, when four kings held the birth name Mentuhotep ("Montu is content"). Thereafter Amun took over as the principal Theban deity and also became the pre-eminent god in the Egyptian pantheon. Both were eventually merged with the Sun God, becoming Amun-Re and Montu-Re respectively.

Opposite: Obelisk at Karnak, dedicated to the Eighteenth Dynasty king Tuthmosis I. Although his reign was relatively brief, around twelve years, Tuthmosis I pursued an aggressive foreign policy which resulted in Egypt's sphere of influence stretching farther than ever before. Accounts of great military victories were recorded for posterity on temple walls, showing a clear link between religious and secular life. The king was both high priest and army commander, and vanquishing Egypt's enemies was seen as vital to maintain order or maat. *Battles were fought in the name of the gods, who granted victories and in turn had military triumphs dedicated to them.*

Above: The Great Hypostyle Hall at Karnak, often listed in ancient times as one of the Wonders of the World. It forms part of the temple complex dedicated to Amun and was the work of a number of pharaohs: begun during the Eighteenth Dynasty and completed under the Ramessids. This vast space—334ft by 174ft— was once an open courtyard. It was originally roofed in by huge sandstone slabs, the only natural light coming from 65ft-high clerestory windows. This was in marked contrast to the Amarna period, when religious ceremonies were conducted in open rather than enclosed spaces. The roof was supported by a dense forest of 134 columns, twelve of which end in open papyrus flowers, the remainder being in closed-bud style. These symbolized the papyrus reeds which grew in the primal swamp from which life emerged, according to the creation myth. Temple complexes also usually included a sacred lake to represent the chaotic waters from which order sprang.

Above: Relief carvings at Karnak. These are in raised relief, where the background has been cut away to create the desired image. Sunk relief, where the figures are cut directly from the stone, was a particular feature of the Amarna period. Before the heretic king Amenhotep IV changed his name to Akhenaten and established a new capital near modern Tell el-Amarna he built four temples at Karnak, all dedicated to the solar deity the Aten.

Above: *Relief from the Red Chapel of Hatshepsut at Karnak, showing the queen burning incense in honor of the gods. Hatshepsut was the half-sister and wife of Tuthmosis II. On the king's early death Hatshepsut ruled as regent on behalf of the young Tuthmosis III. She was not the first female pharaoh, but a reign of twenty years marks her out among the women who sat on Egypt's throne.*

Right: *Queen Hatshepsut depicted in sphinx form. She was invariably shown wearing the false beard, nemes headcloth and uraeus, the regalia of kingship.*

Opposite: *Relief from an obelisk at Karnak, showing Hatshepsut, in masculine form, being crowned by Amun. After acting as regent for Tuthmosis III for seven years, Hatshepsut took the title "Son of Re" and declared herself king. She also promoted the idea that she was of divine birth, Amun having taken her father's form and impregnated her mother. The hieroglyphs relating to Amun were defaced during Akhenaten's reign and restored later.*

Right: Relief from the Red Chapel of Hatshepsut, showing the queen with Seshat, goddess of writing. During Hatshepsut's reign there were several trading expeditions to the land of Punt—possibly modern Somalia—which were recorded on the walls of her mortuary temple at Deir el-Bahri. Gold was among the items brought back, and the reliefs show Seshat recording the weight of the precious cargo.

Below: Hapshepsut and Amun, in the form of the ancient ithyphallic fertility god Min. By the New Kingdom Min had merged with Amun. Royal coronations and jubilee celebrations usually included a festival of Min to guarantee the pharaoh's potency.

Right: Statue of Neferure, daughter of Tuthmosis II and Hatshepsut, and her tutor, Senenmut. Mystery surrounds the fate of Hatshepsut, Neferure, and Senenmut—Hatshepsut's chief advisor—and their disappearance may have cleared the way for Tuthmosis III to finally get his hands on the reins of power. The new king removed Hatshepsut's name from some monuments and destroyed the Red Chapel. It was once thought this was retribution for the long period in which he was denied his rightful place on the throne. Modern scholars believe that Hatshepsut and Tuthmosis III enjoyed a successful coregency, and that the king's subsequent actions had more to do with maintaining the tradition of male rule rather than a desire for revenge.

Hieroglyphs

Hieroglyphs—literally "to carve in stone"—date from the beginning of the Dynastic era, around 3100 BC, and were in use until the fourth century AD. Fewer than a thousand hieroglyphs were used during the Pharaonic period. Of these, some stood for words, some for sounds, others for complete ideas. For example, a boat hieroglyph represented exactly what it depicted, but if there was no sail it also stood for the concept of "north," the direction of the Nile current. There was no punctuation or indication of where words or sentences began or ended. Hieroglyphs were usually read from right to left, except when a symmetrical form was required for inscriptions on either side of a stela.

To the Ancient Egyptians writing and art were interconnected: wall paintings could be regarded as largescale hieroglyphs; hieroglyphs as artistic images in miniature. Hieroglyphs retained their importance as a sacred means of communication; indeed the Egyptians believed this form to be a gift from Thoth, the moon god. But by around 2700 BC hieratic script was introduced for mundane tasks such as business accounts. This was a cursive form of hieroglyphs, the shapes more akin to letters. Over time hieratic script itself began to vary, from careful calligraphy for more important work to a faster, functional form where neither embellishment nor longevity was required. During the Late period the latter had developed into a separate form known as demotic script.

By the fourth century AD Egypt had converted to Christianity and adopted the Greek alphabet and Coptic script. The country's traditional forms of writing were deemed unsuitable for Christian texts and fell into disuse. Hieroglyphs remained a mystery for some 1400 years before the French scholar Jean-François Champollion found the key to deciphering them.

Opposite: *The Temple of Luxor, dedicated to Amun, was begun during the Middle Kingdom but it was Amenhotep III who was chiefly responsible for creating the complex as it is today. Its main purpose was as a setting for the annual* opet *festival, when a cult statue of Amun was borne from Karnak to Luxor. This ceremonial procession was associated with fertility, of both Amun and, by extension, the reigning pharaoh.*

Above: *One of two huge seated statues of Amenhotep III, known as the Colossi of Memnon. Situated on the west bank at Thebes, these 59ft-high quartzite sandstone statues once stood at the entrance to Amenhotep III's mortuary temple, though little of this remains today. At the king's feet are the diminutive figures of his mother, Mutemwiya, and wife, Queen Tiy.*

Opposite: Statuette of the god Amun, from the temple dedicated to him at Karnak. Like the other Egyptian deities, Amun was associated with an animal: the ram, famed for its virility and belligerence. However, Amun was always depicted in human form.

Above: Fragment of an Eighteenth Dynasty relief at Saqqara showing a woman bearing offerings.

Right: Detail of a relief from the Temple of Hatshepsut, on the west bank at Thebes. Religious festivals were times of great merry-making, with music and dance playing a central role. Dancing could be purely for entertainment purposes but it also had a ritual element, for example in funeral processions. Little distinction was made between rhythmic dance and what today would be called acrobatic or gymnastic displays.

Opposite: Rameses II, third king of the Nineteenth Dynasty, who reigned for sixty-six years. He oversaw some magnificent architectural achievements, including the Ramasseum, his mortuary temple at western Thebes, and two rock-hewn temples at Abu Simbel in Nubia. Rameses II also made several additions to the Temple of Amun at Luxor, including the great monumental gateway, the First Pylon. For this work he ordered that stone from the temples dedicated to the discredited Aten at Karnak be used. Rameses II often usurped the work of his forebears, superimposing his own cartouches over those of former kings and replacing their statues with his own.

Above: Relief from the Temple of Rameses II at Luxor, showing a procession forming part of the annual opet *festival. The other main Theban festival in honor of Amun involved a procession bearing cult statues from Karnak across the Nile to the Temple of Nebheptra Mentuhotep, situated on the west bank. This was known as the Valley Festival.*

Left: Painted relief at Karnak.

Opposite: Seshat, the goddess of writing, depicted wearing her characteristic headdress of inverted cow horns atop a flower. Seshat was a royal chronicler, not a deity of the people. New Kingdom reliefs show her inscribing the leaves of the ished tree with details of the pharaoh's reign, and she also assisted the king in marking out the ground prior to temple construction work.

Left: Hieroglyph representing the crested ibis, which was used to express the word "akh". Egyptians believed that a person's ba *and* ka—*roughly equating to personality and spirit—had to be reunited after death before a person could successfully take his place in the Underworld. The* akh *was the result of this union, and once accomplished was fixed for eternity.*

Below: King-list from the temple of Rameses II at Abydos. It records Rameses' offerings to his predecessors, whose names are recorded in rows of cartouches. All incumbent kings did this as a means of establishing their own legitimacy in the royal line. The kings associated with the Amarna period of the previous dynasty were omitted from the list.

Above: From the Early Dynastic era the ram was a potent symbol, with its obvious connection with fertility. Several gods were depicted in the form of a ram, the most important of whom was Khnum, whose chief cult center was the island of Elephantine, near modern Aswan. According to the Elephantine creation myth Khnum fashioned the other deities and mankind on his potter's wheel. After Amun's ascent to become king of the gods he too adopted the ram as his sacred symbol. This line of ramheaded sphinxes stands guard over the Temple of Amun at Karnak.

Opposite: Hieroglyphs and the cartouche of Rameses II at the Temple of Luxor. Reliefs on the First Pylon, built by Rameses, describe his great victory over the Hittites in the Levant, modern Syria-Palestine. The Egyptian view of kingship demanded that the king be portrayed vanquishing the enemy; in fact the Battle of Qadesh ended in stalemate, and Rameses married two Hittite princesses by way of consolidating an uneasy peace between the warring peoples.

Above: The magnificent funerary temple of the Eighteenth Dynasty queen Hatshepsut at Deir el-Bahri. It was partly cut into the Theban cliffs but with three freestanding terraces, each approached by a ramp. Hatshepsut was not the first female pharaoh but her twenty-one-year rule, initially as regent for her stepson, Tuthmosis III, was unprecedented. Hatshepsut proclaimed herself pharaoh after a seven-year period as regent, legitimizing the move by asserting that she was the daughter of Amun. The walls of the temple show the Amun and the cow goddess Hathor endorsing Hatshepsut as Egypt's ruler. However, she is regarded as a "female king" rather than queen, since the concept of a female pharaoh contravened the concept of maat, *or natural order. It was for this reason that her successor, Tuthmosis III, removed her name from king-lists.*

Above: Relief from the island of Elephantine at Aswan, chief cult center of the ram god Khnum. He was worshiped as a creator god from the Early Dynastic period, believed to have forged mankind on his potter's wheel. Egyptians believed the annual inundation began on Elephantine, and Khnum was thus associated with the fertility of the land. When the Nile waters failed to produce a rich harvest it was to Khnum that appeals and offerings were made. The margins were perilously thin: a 26ft rise at the First Cataract at Aswan assured a bountiful food supply; 3ft less meant a lean year, while 19ft would have led to famine once surpluses were exhausted.

Right: Wall scene from Medinet Habu, the funerary temple of the Twentieth Dynasty king Rameses III, situated on Thebes' west bank. The last great New Kingdom pharaoh, Rameses III led Egypt to famous victories over the Libyans and a migrant tribe known as the Sea Peoples, events which were recorded at Medinet Habu. Other scenes show the king at leisure with members of his harem, and it is believed that a plot to assassinate the king was hatched among the royal concubines. There is doubt as to whether the plan was successful, but the plotters were put to death. Even if the aged king survived the attempt on his life, his reign appears to have petered out amid considerable internal strife.

Right: Detail of a relief showing Akhenaten, with typically spindly fingers, dropping unguent onto an offering to the Aten. In the first year of his reign, as Amenhotep IV, he dedicated a new temple to the Aten at Karnak, the center of worship of the god Amun and where Egypt's most powerful priesthood resided. This was the first step toward imposing a new state religion on the country.

Opposite: This 13ft-high sandstone statue of Akhenaten adorned the Gempaaten temple site at Karnak. Akhenaten ordered temples dedicated to other gods to be closed, which would have impacted severely on Egypt's economy as well as revolutionizing the country's theological base.

The Heretic King

During the reign of Amenhotep III, the Eighteenth Dynasty's ninth king, there was burgeoning interest in the cult of the Aten. Like Re, the Aten was a solar deity who had held a minor position in the Egyptian pantheon for centuries. The Aten was a purer manifestation of the sun, represented by a simple solar disk. Temples dedicated to the Aten were erected, but it was the royal court taking the lead, not the priesthood. Indeed, Amenhotep's endorsement of the Aten may have in part been motivated by a desire to curb the power of the Karnak priests. Although the king placed the Aten at the top of the religious hierarchy— ahead of both Amun-Re, the Theban manifestation of the solar deity, and Atum, the creator god of the Heliopolitan myth—he took no steps to disseminate the new theological order throughout the country.

The cult of the Aten reached a pinnacle during the reign of his son, Amenhotep IV. The Aten was declared the sole creator god and temples honoring other deities were closed as Egypt for the first time embraced monotheism. In the fifth year of his reign Amenhotep IV changed his name to Akhenaten —"Glorious is the Aten"—and established a new capital at a virgin site 186 miles north of Thebes. The revolutionary regime did not survive Akhenaten's death, some eighteen years later. Under Tutankhamun the royal court returned to Thebes, with Amun reinstated as the pre-eminent deity. Akhenaten was now regarded as a heretic and all references to him and the Aten were expunged from the records.

Children and Childbirth

Unsurprisingly, the mysteries of pregnancy and childbirth were surrounded by ritual and superstition. There were many fertility rituals, including women exposing their genitalia before a statue of Hathor, one of the gods associated with childbirth. Once pregnancy was achieved one method for predicting the outcome involved urinating onto barley and wheat. If the wheat grew a boy would be delivered; barley would bring forth a girl. If neither flourished there would be no child. Irrespective of such superstitious practices stillbirths were indeed common, as was infant mortality and the death of the mother in childbirth.

Incantations were recited during delivery, and wands carved with images of gods thought to offer protection during labor were used. As well as Hathor these included Bes and Taweret, the latter often depicted as a pregnant hippopotamus. On a more practical level poppy seeds crushed in beer were used for pain relief. During delivery women either squatted on bricks or used a wooden birthing stool.

The day of the month on which a child entered the world was thought to determine the manner in which he or she would leave it. For example, a child born on the 4th would succumb to fever, one born on the 23rd would be carried off by a crocodile. Other days were benign, associated with respect and longevity. A child's first utterances were also thought to be critical in determining whether it would survive infancy.

The onset of puberty was the point at which childhood ended and adulthood began; the Egyptians had no concept of adolescence. This rite of passage was marked by the removal of the sidelock of hair which was often worn by children.

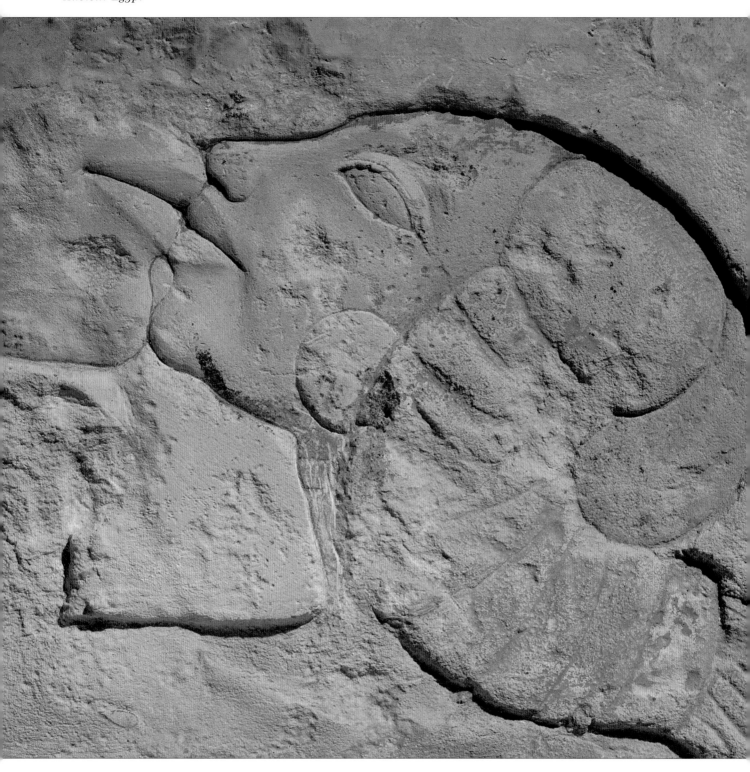

Above: Detail of a relief showing Nefertiti kissing one of her six daughters, possibly Merytaten. In the latter years of Akhenaten's reign Nefertiti's role as principal wife was usurped and the considerable power and influence she had wielded was curtailed. One school of thought is that Nefertiti died in the fourteenth year of Akhenaten's reign. Others suggest that with no male heir she assumed the role of coregent and on her husband's death acceded to the throne as Smenkhkare.

Opposite: Unfinished quartzite head of Queen Nefertiti, which would have been completed with a majestic headdress in a different material. It is the work of the foremost sculptor of the period, Tuthmose, whose studio at el-Amarna was discovered in 1912 by the German archeologist Ludwig Borchardt. The centerpiece of this stunning collection was the painted bust of Nefertiti (overleaf). Although the inlaid pigment of one eye was missing, this breathtaking piece became one of Ancient Egypt's great icons.

Opposite: Nefertiti, principal wife of the Eighteenth Dynasty king Akhenaten. Famed for her beauty, Nefertiti wielded enormous power during Egypt's short-lived flirtation with monotheism in what is now known as the Amarna period.

Right: Detail of a relief showing Akhenaten offering an olive branch to the Aten. The sun disk's rays had hands at their extremities, some of which held the ankh, *the sign of life.*

Art of the Amarna Period

Akhenaten's determination to break with the past and previous conventions can clearly be seen in the artistic output of the period. When the royal court relocated to Amarna the king took with him craftsmen who were encouraged to break with tradition, notably in the depiction of the human body. Idealism disappeared, and the new form of expression can be seen most strikingly in images of Akhenaten himself, who was portrayed with an elongated head and neck, sometimes exaggerated by the addition of a tall headdress. Parts of his body were swollen and distended, others spindly and emaciated. Whether this was an accurate portrayal—one theory propounds that Akhenaten suffered from a glandular disorder—or simply a new convention is unclear, as his body has never been found. However, all human figures were depicted in this distinctive style, suggesting that every Egyptian ought to conform to the image of the god-king.

The scenes depicting the royal family were far more intimate and personal than any of the earlier dynastic period. For example, Akhenaten and Nefertiti might be shown kissing their children or presenting them with gifts.

The Aten also featured prominently, represented as a solar disk with rays in the form of outstretched hands. Some of the hands proffered the *ankh*—the sign of life associated with royal and divine power—to the king and his family. This reinforced the view that ordinary Egyptians had no direct interaction with the Aten; they worshiped Akhenaten, who was the conduit between them and the sole creator god.

Above: Detail of a relief showing two of the princesses born to Akhenaten and Nefertiti. One of the features of the art of the Amarna period is the prominence given to the royal children. The symbolic rays of the sun disk were often depicted shining on the entire royal family, not simply the pharaoh. Ordinary Egyptians could only worship the Aten indirectly, through shrines to the king and his family.

Opposite: Bust of one of Akhenaten and Nefertiti's daughters. Akhenaten married their third-born, Ankhesenpaaten, in a failed attempt to secure a male heir. She later became the wife of the boy-king Tutankhaten, in whose reign the cult of the Aten was abandoned and the traditional deities restored. The royal court returned to Memphis and both replaced the "aten" suffix to their names with "amun," thereby distancing themselves from the former regime.

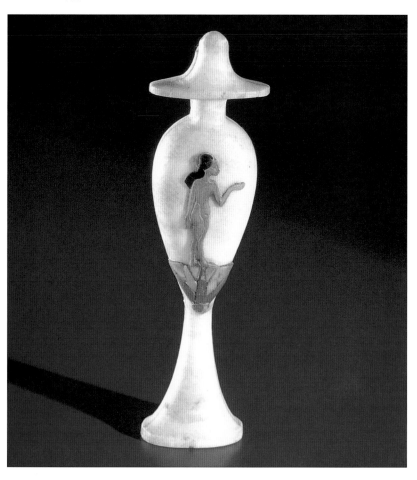

Left: Alabaster perfume bottle, inlaid with carnelian, obsidian, and colored glass. It depicts a naked Armana princess making an offering to the Aten. After Akhenaten's eighteen-year reign the throne passed to the shadowy figure of Smenkhkare, whom some believe may have been Queen Nefertiti. Another school of thought is that Smenkhkare was a young prince of uncertain parentage who died when he was around twenty, the throne passing to his younger brother, Tutankhamun.

Below: Fragment of a relief showing head and shoulders in typical Amarna style: thin, elongated neck and full lips. The revolutionary artistic conventions of the period died out with the regime which spawned it.

Above: Ivory panel from the Amarna period showing one of the princesses picking lotus flowers and grapes.

Above: Nefertiti offers libation to the Aten. She was also depicted smiting Egypt's foes, an image usually associated with the pharaoh, and officiating in state ceremonies alongside her husband. Having played such an active role in the revolutionary regime, Nefertiti suffered the same fate as Akhenaten when the old order was restored. Images of both were defaced, and their names obliterated from public records.

Right: Relief depicting a member of the royal family receiving the beneficent rays of the Aten.

Opposite: Fragment of a sunk relief showing scribes rendering accounts. Akhenaten's preoccupation with the cult of the Aten contributed toward a period of economic decline, which in turn caused internal disorder and a weakening of royal authority.

Trade

Egypt was the wealthiest country of the ancient world, but until the Late period it operated a nonmonetary economy. A barter system was used for both domestic and foreign trade. Wages and taxes were also paid in produce. At its simplest level this system involved two parties adding to or removing goods to be bartered until each was satisfied and a deal was struck. The vendor may or may not have wanted what he took in exchange. In the latter case he would have wanted to insure that the goods received could be used in a future transaction. This was an unwieldy system and by the New Kingdom —possibly earlier—a transaction system based on copper weights was introduced for low-value items, with silver and gold used for more expensive goods.

Egypt was largely self-sufficient but it did look beyond its shores for certain goods: cedarwood from Lebanon; lapis lazuli from Afghanistan; ebony and ivory from central Africa; silver and bronze from Syria; olive oil from Crete. Egypt's large gold reserves were often used for exchange purposes.

Particularly at the height of the country's imperial power goods were often received as diplomatic gifts or tribute. The first coinage appeared during the Twenty-fifth Dynasty, c. 400 BC, the precursor to the introduction of a full monetary economy during the Ptolemaic period.

Army Life and Weaponry

The fact that Egypt maintained its autonomy for some three millennia, despite the covetous eyes that were cast in its direction by outsiders, bears testament to the country's military strength. Egypt's geography certainly helped: desert on three fronts severely restricted the points of possible incursion.

The country's borders were breached in the Second Intermediate period by the Hyksos, who controlled the northern region for a century before being driven out. Prior to this there was no standing army; during the Old Kingdom men were conscripted as and when needed, and these were sometimes regional rather than national forces. The dagger, sword, spear, battleaxe, and bow and arrow were the chief weapons of the Early Dynastic era. There was no armor apart from shields, which were made of either wood or leather stretched over wooden bracing.

Egypt learned the salutary lesson of the Hyksos invasion. Afterwards there was a professional army and an expansionist mind-set. There was also new weaponry, some of which was certainly a legacy of the Hyksos period. This included the horse and chariot, the composite bow, and helmets. Mailcoats also appeared, bronze plates riveted to leather tunics. Chariots were manned by two soldiers, a driver and an archer, who were soon regarded as the army's élite troops.

Logistics were vital to the army's effectiveness, and scribes meticulously oversaw the vast supplies needed to keep an army on the move. As in other areas of the economy the army operated on a barter or voucher system. Rations were allocated according to rank, the troops receiving vouchers which could be exchanged for food.

Soldiers wounded in battle often succumbed to their injuries. Honey was used as both a disinfectant and antibiotic but blood loss and infection still accounted for many deaths. Those who covered themselves in glory could win the golden fly medal, while conscripted slaves could gain their freedom through sterling military service.

Opposite: Preparatory drawing for a tomb relief depicting a horse and chariot.

Above: Detail from the magnificent painted wooden casket found in Tutankhamun's tomb. It shows the horse-drawn chariot, which arrived in Egypt during the Second Intermediate period, c. 1650–c. 1550 BC. As a fast-moving platform from which archers could fire their arrows, the chariot quickly became an important part of Egypt's military capability. Indeed, the soldiers who manned the chariots were the army's élite troops, known as the maryannu. *Ornate ceremonial chariots also became part of the royal regalia.*

Right: Amarna tomb relief showing soldiers in battle mode. It has been suggested that Akhenaten had little interest in foreign policy and allowed Egypt's grip on Near Eastern territories over which she had dominion to be loosened. The iconography supports this view, for there is little evidence indicating that Akhenaten was a warrior-king. However, other sources do refer to campaigns in western Asia, and the fact that these are under-represented pictorially may simply be yet another convention of the period.

The Valley of the Kings

The beginning of the New Kingdom, c. 1550 BC, marked the dawn of a new age of unity in Egypt as the Hyksos invaders were finally driven out after a century of occupation. It also saw the establishment of a new royal necropolis on the west bank of the Nile at Thebes, a short distance from modern Luxor. The pyramid age was over; New Kingdom pharaohs would be interred in tombs cut into remote cliffs in the desert valley. Tuthmosis I, the third Eighteenth Dynasty ruler, was the first to be buried in what is known as the Valley of the Kings. Rameses XI, the final Twentieth Dynasty pharaoh, was the sixty-second and last person to be entombed there.

Security concerns may well have informed the decision to site the necropolis in terrain less accessible to tomb-robbers. The fact that it was near Thebes, Egypt's most important religious and administrative center, was undoubtedly another factor. It has been suggested that the very topography of the area may also have been an issue. From a distance the cliffs resembled the shape of the hieroglyph for "horizon": a solar disk emerging between two mountains. As the sun disappeared over the horizon to be born anew the next morning, the Egyptians associated the western skyline with death and rebirth. It was thus a fitting place for the end of mortal existence and the beginning of the afterlife.

The walls of the tombs were elaborately decorated with images and funerary texts whose purpose was to insure the pharaoh's safe passage on the journey to join the deities. This was in marked contrast to the pyramid age, when the walls were generally undecorated. Another difference, enforced due to the difficult terrain, was that the mortuary and valley temples were constructed some distance away, on the edge of the desert. By the end of the Twenty-first Dynasty steps were taken to dismantle the Valley of the Kings, probably because of the attentions of grave- robbers. This program included removing many of the mummified pharaohs to Deir el-Bahri, while others were placed in the tomb of Amenhotep II. Both caches were discovered in the late nineteenth century.

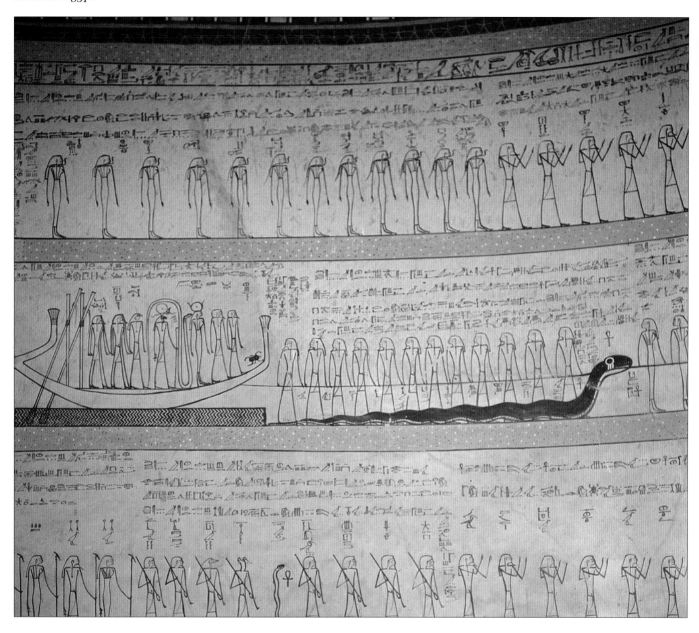

Above: Painted scene from the wall of Tuthmosis III's tomb in the Valley of the Kings. The images are from the Amduat, the book of "that which is in the netherworld." This covered a number of funerary texts describing the Sun God's journey through the night sky and rebirth at the new dawn. It also contained spells which protected the deceased king on his journey to the afterlife.

Opposite: Detail of a wall painting from the tomb of the Eighteenth Dynasty king Tuthmosis IV, showing the king being received into the afterlife by Hathor. The cow goddess offers Tuthmosis the ankh, the sign of life. This was a recurring image, indicating that the king had left the mortal world to begin eternal life among the gods. Tuthmosis IV, son of Amenhotep II, does not appear to have been the chosen heir. He was promised the throne if he cleared away the sand covering the Great Sphinx at Giza, the request coming from the creator god in the form of a dream. Tuthmosis carried out this wish and duly acceded to the the throne, reigning c.1400–c. 1390 BC.

Above: Head of Queen Tiy, principal wife of Amenhotep III and mother of the heretic king Akhenaten. Tiy did not come from the inner royal circle, and her elevation through marriage represented a break with convention. She played an active political role, which included promoting with Amenhotep the cult of the Aten at the expense of the established deific order. In doing so the king sought to emasculate the priests of Amun, whom he believed wielded too much power, and his choice of Tiy as principal wife was probably in part motivated by a desire to challenge the authority of the Karnak priesthood.

Opposite: Mummified head of Nebiry, chief of the royal stables during the reign of Tuthmosis III. He was buried in the Valley of the Queens, his tomb among those discovered by Ernesto Schiaparelli during excavation work between 1903 and 1905.

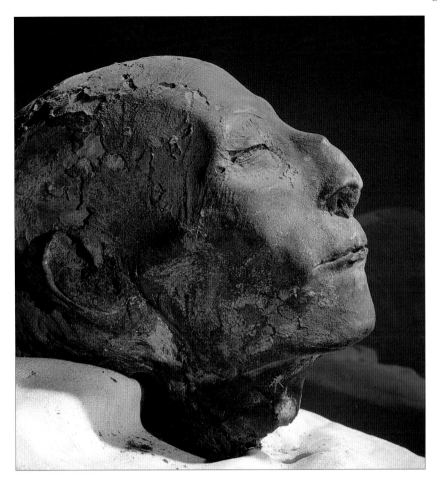

Mummification

The preservation of the body after death was important to the Ancient Egyptians, who believed that a deceased person's *ka* would return to it for sustenance. During the Early Dynastic period bodies dried out naturally in the arid ground of shallow graves. Later, removal of the internal organs prevented the body from decaying from within. Mummification was developed during the Old Kingdom as the ultimate method of preservation, although this elaborate and costly process was available only to kings and the wealthier class. By the Middle Kingdom this practice was much more widespread.

The term derives from the Arabic "*mummiy*a," meaning "bitumen." The resins used sometimes left the body blackened and it was assumed—wrongly— that bitumen had been used. The first stage in the process was cleansing the body in a solution containing the sodium compound natron. After evisceration the body was soaked in natron for forty days. It was stuffed with sawdust, leaves and other dry material so that the body shape was maintained. If a

body part was missing a replacement was fashioned to give the semblance of completeness. After coating the body in resin it was then ready for bandaging, which was carried out by specialists under the guidance of the *hery seshta* (controller of the mysteries). The latter took overall charge of the embalming process and probably wore a jackal mask to represent Anubis, the god associated with the preservation ritual. The bandaging process took fifteen days and used over 300 square yards of linen. Amulets were packed within the layers to give protection on the journey to the afterlife. The most important of these was the heart scarab, placed over the breast, which would help bring a favorable outcome in the Weighing of the Heart ceremony. Incantations of spells by lector-priests fulfilled a similar function.

The entire mummification process, from death to burial, took seventy days. This is thought to be significant, mirroring the phase of the dog star Sirius, on which the Ancient Egyptian calendar was based.

Carter's Discovery

Howard Carter and Lord Carnarvon began their first season of excavation work in 1907. The ensuing years yielded many minor triumphs, including the discovery of temples dedicated to Queen Hatshepsut and Rameses IV, but their long-cherished aim was to carry out excavation work in the Valley of the Kings. However, they were prevented from doing so until 1915 when the American Theodore Davis relinquished the concession, allowing Carter and Carnarvon to begin work at the royal necropolis.

By 1921 Carnarvon had reached the conclusion that the discoveries made thus far had not been worth the investment of time and money. Believing that Davis may have been right all along and the Valley of the Kings had yielded all its secrets, Carnarvon prepared to withdraw. Carter convinced his sponsor to continue for one more season. On November 4 1922 a rock-cut step below the entrance to the tomb of Rameses VI was found. The sunken steps led to a walled-up tomb entrance. A telegram was hastily dispatched to Carnarvon, who arrived in Egypt on November 23. Work resumed, and the excitement grew as cartouches containing Tutankhamun's name were uncovered.

On November 26 Carter made a small opening and prepared to enter the chamber. There was evidence that it had been entered and resealed, but the treasure was intact. Carter later recorded, "At first I could see nothing, the hot air escaping from the chamber causing the candle flame to flicker, but presently, as my eyes grew accustomed to the light, details of the room within emerged slowly from the mist, strange animals, statues and gold—everywhere the glint of gold." Among the myriad treasures was the quartzite sarcophagus, three anthropoidal coffins, the innermost of solid gold. This contained the mummy of the king, which had lain undisturbed for over 3000 years.

Opposite: Hunting scene from one of the chests found in Tutankhamun's tomb, showing the king in action, with Queen Ankhesenamun looking on. Many objects recovered from the chests were associated with such manly pursuits befitting an Egyptian ruler. These included slings, clubs, boomerangs, throwsticks, swords, and archery equipment. For defensive purposes there were eight shields, some for ceremonial use, others that would have seen service on the battlefield. The ceremonial shields depict Tutankhamun as warrior-king, either in lion form, trampling on Egypt's enemies, or in human form, smiting the foe with a falchion.

Above: Detail from the wooden casket found in the antechamber of Tutankhamun's tomb, which bore exquisitely painted hunting and battle scenes. It shows the Nubians being crushed by the king. The jumble of bodies of the vanquished also suggests chaos, out of which Tutankhamun has brought order.

Above: Detail of the golden shrine found in the antechamber of Tutankhamun's tomb. It was adorned with numerous delicate sunk reliefs showing scenes of the royal couple's daily life. The shrine originally contained a statuette which was plundered in antiquity. Grave-robbers twice gained entry to the tomb; on the second occasion they were apprehended, and their haul retrieved and thrown back into the chamber.

Opposite: Panel from the back of the golden throne of Tutankhamun, showing Queen Ankhesenamun offering her husband perfume or ointment from a salve-cup. This touching scene also encapsulates the fraught politico-religious situation toward the end of the Amarna period. The sun-disk image is pure Atenism, yet in some of the cartouches the "aten" element has been replaced by "amun." Such overt references to a period condemned as heretical often brought defacement. There were traces of a linen covering on the throne when it was discovered, possibly suggesting that it was thought too valuable to destroy, but its association with the discredited regime meant that it could not be prominently displayed.

Left: Tutankhamun is embraced by Osiris, god of the Underworld. Osiris wears the atef, *a tall white crown flanked by two plumes. His flesh was sometimes white, matching his robe, or green, to symbolize regeneration.*

Right: A scene from the north wall of Tutankhamun's burial chamber, showing Ay, clad in the leopard skin of the sem *priest, performing the Opening of the Mouth ceremony on the dead king. This ritual was usually conducted by the son and heir but when there was a succession problem—as was the case after Tutankhamun's death—it was also a way for the new king to legitimize his position.*

Opening of the Mouth Ceremony

This was a vital part of the funerary ritual, dating back to the Predynastic era, in which the deceased's faculties were restored. The mouth and other areas of the body associated with the senses were touched with a range of special instruments. The ceremony, which was performed on either the mummified body or the funerary statue, allowed the person to receive the sustenance necessary for survival in the afterlife. Only then was the body able to become the vessel for the *ka*, or spirit, which survived death. The Egyptians believed it was then reunited with the person's *ba*, the non-physical part of an individual's makeup, roughly equating to the concept of personality. The *ba* was thought to roam freely during the day, returning to the tomb by night. The union of the *ka* and *ba* produced the *akh*, the form in which the dead enjoyed eternal life in the Underworld.

Carvings depicting Tutankhamun (opposite) and Queen Ankhesenamun (above). Tutankhamun left no
natural heir and was buried with two stillborn children and a lock of hair belonging to his grandmother,
Queen Tiy. His successor to the throne, Ay, was a court advisor and commoner. He secured his position
by marrying the royal widow.

Opposite left: One of a number of magnificent pectorals recovered from Tutankhamun's tomb. The straps are formed from inlaid plaques with uraei, scarabs, and solar disks. The pendant has a scarab holding the sun aloft, flanked by two uraei. The uraeus was the cobra image which was associated with kingship and featured in most royal headdresses. Wadjyt, the cobra goddess, represented Lower Egypt, while Upper Egypt was represented by the vulture goddess Nekhbet. The cobra and vulture both appeared in the royal titulary and regalia to identify the king as ruler of the two lands.

Opposite right: A pendant of gold in the form of the goddess Werethekau with the body of a serpent suckling the child-king Tutankhamun.

Left: A detail from the chariot of Tutankhamun. A gilded wood figure of Horus Falcon bears on his head the sun disk decorated with a winged Khephri, the scarab god asscociated with the sun.

Tutankhamun

Tutankhamun was the only known son of the New Kingdom pharaoh Akhenaten, during whose reign all gods were proscribed as Egypt embraced monotheism in the shape of the solar deity, the Aten. He was probably born at Akhentaten, the capital city founded by Akhenaten at the birth of the revolutionary regime, near modern el-Amarna. Tutankhaten, as he was then known (meaning "living image of the Aten"), came to the throne c. 1333 BC, when he was about eight years old. During his reign the royal court returned to Memphis, while Thebes was once again established as Egypt's most important religious site; worship of the Aten to the exclusion of all other deities was now condemned as heretical. The boy-king was but a pawn in the unraveling of the regime,

falling prey to senior court advisors. He did embrace a return to theological orthodoxy by changing his name to Tutankhamun, thereby distancing himself from the cult of the Aten.

Following Tutankhamun's death, at the age of sixteen or seventeen, he quickly faded into obscurity. His association with the heresy perpetrated by his father was enough to insure his name was obliterated from king-lists produced by the Ramessid rulers of the following two centuries. When the Valley of the Kings was abandoned during the reign of Rameses X1 (c. 1099–c.1069 BC) and the tombs dismantled, that of Tutankhamun was overlooked. Its spectacular treasures lay undisturbed for over three millennia until Howard Carter's famous discovery in 1922, when this largely unknown Eighteenth Dynasty pharaoh became a household name the world over.

Tutankhamun's Curse

On April 5 1923, just five months after the discovery of Tutankhamun's tomb, Lord Carnarvon died from an infected mosquito bite. He was fifty-eight. Newspaper reports quickly leaped on the idea of a mummy seeking revenge on those who had violated its resting place, which naturally made excellent copy. The curse of the mummy had already entered the vernacular in Gothic horror stories, and Hollywood soon jumped on the bandwagon. The media seized on further deaths of those who had been members of Howard Carter's team or visited the tomb. These included Carter's associate Arthur Mace, who at the time of the discovery was already suffering from pleurisy, and French Egyptologist Georges Benedite, who died from a fall having recently been to the tomb. Carnarvon's brother, Aubrey Herbert, an X-ray specialist, died suddenly in September 1923 while on his way to examine the mummy. Not only were there perfectly rational explanations for virtually all of the deaths—for example, Lord Carnarvon's constitution had been weak and death from an infected mosquito bite was by no means uncommon—but several of the twenty-six-strong party present at the opening of the tomb lived well into their eighties. This, of course, was glossed over by those who preferred to believe malevolent forces were at work—and by those interested in newspaper circulation figures.

Opposite: Perfume jar from Tutankhamun's burial chamber. Although the king was interred with many magnificent pieces, and the tomb was the best-preserved of any discovered thus far, the burial chamber itself was small. This suggests that his chosen burial site may not have been ready by the time of his premature death and a substitute was hastily found.

Above: A detail of the gilt shrine of Tutankhamun which originally contained statuettes of the royal couple. The scene depicts a ritual hunting scene in which Queen Ankhesenamun helps her husband.

Left: A pendant from the tomb of Tutankhamun. The king's mummy was decorated with over 100 pieces of jewelry.

Overleaf: Wall painting from the tomb of Horemheb, a former army commander who rose to become a senior official during Tutankhamun's reign, and eventually pharaoh. It was during Horemheb's reign that all references to Akhenaten and the heresies of the Amarna period were eradicated. The new ruler even backdated his reign to the death of Amenhotep III in order to expunge this discredited era from the records. A tomb had been prepared for Horemheb at Saqqara, but following his accession to the throne this was abandoned in favor of a more exalted resting place in the Valley of the Kings.

Valley of the Queens

During the Eighteenth Dynasty the Valley of the Kings also accommodated some of the royal wives and princes. These included Queen Tiy, chief wife of Amenhotep III, and Hatshepsut, the wife and half-sister of Tuthmosis II who proclaimed herself pharaoh after his death. Around this time a separate burial site was established on the west bank at Thebes for the upper strata of Egyptian society. But by the Nineteenth Dynasty and throughout the Ramessid period this necropolis was used for the queens and royal children, and to Egyptologists it became known as the Valley of the Queens. At the same time the Valley of the Kings became the exclusive preserve of the pharaohs.

The Valley of the Queens, which houses some seventy-five tombs, was partially excavated in the early eighteenth century, but it was not until 1903 that the site was investigated thoroughly. Italian Egyptologist Ernesto Schiaparelli spent two years there, during which time he made some spectacular discoveries. Probably the most famous of these came in 1904, when Schiaparelli lighted upon the tomb of Nefertari, chief wife of Rameses II. Although the tomb was plundered in antiquity, its painted stucco walls, depicting Nefertari with many of the deities, are magnificent. Many of the scenes reflect the Heliopolitan creation myth which has obvious symbolic resonance: Nefertari hoping to emulate Osiris, who was restored to life after being murdered by his brother Seth.

Right: Wall painting from the tomb of Queen Nefertari, showing the union of the gods Re and Osiris, the latter depicted in the form of a ram.

Opposite: Wall painting from Nefertari's tomb, depicting Osiris. According to legend, Osiris once ruled Egypt, and was thus usually shown with the crook and flail, symbols of kingship. His skin was sometimes white, representing the wrappings of the mummified corpse, and sometimes black, signifying the rich dark silt which underpinned Egypt's economy. Here it is green, symbol of regeneration.

Left: Detail from Nefertari's tomb, showing an egret and a falcon. The latter was a sacred bird associated with a number of gods, most notably Horus, son of Osiris. The ruling pharaoh was believed to be the incarnation of Horus.

Below left: Leonine figure from Nefertari's tomb. The lion god Aker guarded the gateway to the Underworld through which the sun passed each day. Lions were thus associated with death and rebirth, as well as kingship.

Below right: Detail from Nefertari's tomb showing Neith, an ancient creator goddess whose cult center was in the delta town of Sais. She was a warrior deity and also associated with weaving. From the Old Kingdom onwards Neith also had a funerary aspect, since she was one of the four deities who watched over the sarcophagus of the murdered Osiris.

Previous pages: Many of the tombs in the Valley of the Queens were sparsely decorated or left unfinished. Nefertari's tomb was a spectacular exception. In this vividly portrayed scene the goddess Isis, wearing the crown usually attributed to the goddess Hathor, leads the queen by the hand.

Left: Detail of a wall painting from the tomb of Amunherkhepshef, one of Rameses III's many sons. It shows Rameses himself confronting the goddess Isis who is wearing the crown usually associated with the goddess Hathor. The fact that father is depicted accompanying son on the journey to the Underworld to meet the funerary deities has prompted speculation that Amunherkhepshef may have died young, possibly as a result of some congenital disease. Hathor was associated with both love and music, but in a funerary context she was known as "Mistress of the West." Hathor was believed to protect the sun after its disappearance over the western skyline, until its rebirth the following morning. The deceased sought the same protection in their passage to the Underworld, and Hathor thus figures prominently in tomb paintings, receiving the dead at the beginning of their journey to everlasting life.

Opposite: Wall painting of Anubis, from the Valley of the Queens tomb of Khaemwaset, son of Rameses III. Trial records of the attempt to assassinate Rameses III by a secondary wife and members of his harem refer to wax images being used to overpower the guards. Many occult beliefs, such as the "evil eye," have their roots in ancient Egyptian superstitions, and Rameses III's mummy became the cinematic template for the horror genre. Some of those found guilty of plotting against the king were executed, while others of higher birth were allowed to commit suicide, in accordance with custom.

Above: Painting from the tomb of Inherka, a foreman who worked on the Valley of the Kings necropolis during the reigns of Rameses III and IV. Of the ten-day week, workers spent eight days toiling and living on site, returning to their family homes at Deir el-Medina for the other two. Wages were paid in the form of food, fuel, clothing, pottery, and cosmetics. On one occasion, delayed payment led to a strike, the first recorded example of a workforce withdrawing its labor.

Law and Order

Law was enforced in the name of Maat, goddess of truth, morality, and justice. As well as being a deity *maat* was also a concept: the order which emerged from chaos at the moment of creation. This included the idea of correct conduct, and wrongdoing was seen as a threat to natural order. Minor civil disputes were settled by ad hoc committees of local dignitaries. There were often no specialist lawyers or judges present; respected citizens who excelled in all manner of fields were deemed qualified to pontificate on legal matters, and precedent played an important part in the rulings given. There is evidence that a post roughly equivalent to a magistrate did exist, however. For the most serious offenses the king was the ultimate arbiter of justice,

but in practice this role was often delegated to the vizier. Suspects were often deemed guilty until proved innocent and torture was regularly applied to extract confessions. Punishments included confiscation of goods, beatings, branding, and dismemberment. The guilty could face exile, but the death penalty could only be sanctioned by the king. If the guilty absconded their families could be punished instead. From the New Kingdom plaintiffs were able to seek divine judgment from an oracle. It is known that statues of the deified pharaoh Amenhotep I were paraded through the streets of Deir el-Medina during certain festivals, and individuals could take the opportunity to present their petitions. The attendant priests would incline the head of the statue to the left or right to signify their decision. Other gods could be petitioned in a similar way.

Nobles' Tombs

During the New Kingdom, as in earlier times, nobles, senior officials, and courtiers were often interred near the ruler they served. Many were buried in tombs cut into the mountains close to the valleys where the royals were laid to rest. These tombs were naturally less ornate than those of the kings, and with more modest funerary equipment. The wall paintings also depicted more mundane scenes of work and leisure, the daily regime of the tomb owner. There were images of mourners bemoaning the loss of a loved one, in contrast to lavish banqueting occasions, with musicians and dancers providing entertainment. It was hoped that inexhaustible supplies of sumptuous food would sustain the deceased in the afterlife; nourishment and food production were thus prominent in tomb imagery. In creating these images the Egyptians believed the mortal existence would be magically perpetuated in the afterlife. Although the purpose was to create a perfect world for the deceased to inhabit and facilitate his passage into it, these scenes also provide a wealth of information regarding work practices, recreational activities, and living conditions during the New Kingdom.

Right: Nineteenth Dynasty tomb at Deir el-Medina, showing Pashedu, a member of the workforce that built the Valley of the Kings, drinking from a pool in the shade of a date palm.

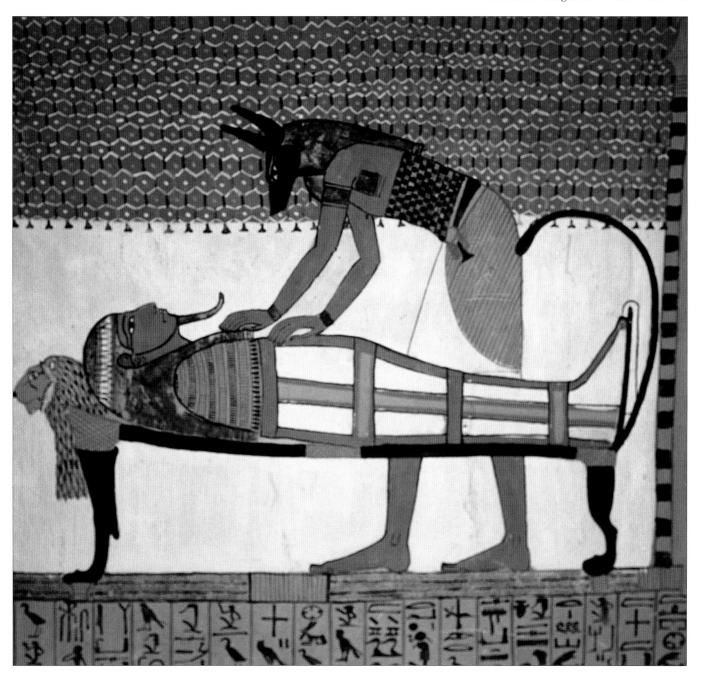

Opposite: Detail from the Nineteenth Dynasty tomb of Sennedjem at Deir el-Medina, the village on Thebes' west bank established during the reign of Tuthmosis I to house the workmen who built the Valley of the Kings. It had its own necropolis, and Sennedjem's tomb is regarded as a masterpiece of its kind. It was discovered in 1886, a perfectly preserved vault in which several members of Sennedjem's family across at least two generations were buried. It is not known what contribution Sennedjem made to the work on the royal tombs in the Valley of the Kings, though he must have enjoyed an elevated status to have warranted such a magnificent private burial chamber. He and his wife, Iineferti, are pictured paying homage to the gods of the Underworld, including Osiris and Horus.

Above: Anubis, the jackal-headed god of embalming and mummification, prepares the body of Sennedjem in its anthropoid coffin. In another scene the mummified Sennedjem is depicted being revivified by the air from the beating wings of hovering kites, just as Osiris was partially restored to life according to legend.

Above: Wall painting from the tomb of Inherkha, showing Underworld deities Anubis and Osiris in front of tables piled high with offerings. The tomb also depicts the demon serpent Apophis, whom the Egyptians believed lay in wait every night to attack the beneficent Sun God. Re withstood the threat by assuming feline form and decapitating the serpent with a knife. Apophis always revived in time to mount a fresh onslaught in this continuing nightly ritual in which good triumphed over evil.

Opposite: Another scene from Inherkha's tomb at Deir el-Medina. Inherkha was a foreman during the reigns of two Twentieth Dynasty rulers, Rameses III and Rameses IV. A priest wearing the mask of Anubis proffers a bowl of water to the mummy, part of the Opening of the Mouth ceremony which would restore the deceased's senses in readiness for the afterlife.

Above: Wall painting from the tomb of the Eighteenth Dynasty official Nebamun at Thebes. In this scene cattle are paraded before the tomb owner, while elsewhere geese are counted to assess Nebamun's wealth. Images of opulence and luxury were used deliberately to create a perfect world for the deceased to enjoy in the afterlife.

Left and opposite: Banqueting scene from the tomb-chapel of Nebamun. Musicians wearing pleated gowns, wigs with lotus blossom, and scented cones on their heads provide the music, one playing the double flute while another claps out a rhythmic accompaniment. Their song is written above them. Dancing girls add to the entertainment by performing before the assembled guests.

Overleaf: Detail from the banqueting scene from Nebamun's tomb, showing one of the guests offering lotus blossom to the nose of another. The lotus was an important symbol of regeneration, and thus highly apposite as a funerary image. According to one of the creation myths, the newborn sun emerged from a lotus flower which was floating on the chaotic waters of Nun. This myth probably grew from the fact that the lotus grew abundantly on the shores of the Nile. It also opened and closed its petals at dawn and dusk respectively, mirroring the diurnal pattern of the sun.

Fashion

Many items of clothing have been found among funerary goods, the oldest being a pleated linen shirt/dress from the Early Dynastic period, c. 2900 BC. Linen, produced from the flax which grew in abundance on the banks of the Nile, was the basic fabric worn by all strata of society. The poor wore simple loincloths, kilts, tunics, or dresses made of coarsely woven linen. The best quality material came from plants which were harvested young and finely spun. The better-off would have embellished their costume with beads, feathers, and belts. These would also have provided color, as textual and artistic references suggest that for a long time linen was left in its natural state. External influences, possibly from those who had migrated to Egypt, promoted the trend toward colored fabrics, and dyeing did eventually become more commonplace. Indigotin was used to produce blue cloth, henna for red, safflower for yellow, and a combination of indigotin and safflower for green.

Clothing was either shaped or of the wrap-around variety. The former involved shaped pieces of fabric, usually triangular or rectangular, sewn together to create a fitted garment. Egyptians also wore headscarves, gloves, and socks, and their regard for good hygiene meant that regularly laundered underwear was important. Until the New Kingdom, when shoes first appeared, the open-toed sandal was the standard item of footwear. Those of the less well-off were made from reeds, the richer wore leather, while the king had a ceremonial golden pair. Accessories included jewelry, such as bracelets, necklaces, and earrings. These sometimes incorporated charms to ward off evil and bring good fortune. For example, children wore fish-shaped amulets to protect them from drowning in the Nile. Wigs and makeup were used by both sexes, both for protection against the sun and for adornment.

Right: Painted scene showing women feasting, from the tomb of Nakht, who was in charge of the royal granaries and vineyards during the reign of Tuthmosis IV.

Weights and Measures

The Egyptians used the decimal system for counting, although there was no symbol for zero or units greater than one. Blanks were used for the former, while the number eight, for example, would be represented by the symbol for one repeated eight times. There was even a symbol for one million, although this may have implied infinity rather than a precise mathematical value.

Length was measured in royal cubits. This was 52.4cm, based on the length of a man's forearm. Craftsmen used wooden cubit rods, while surveyors used rope with knots as distance markers. The unit of area was the *aroura*, equal to 100 cubits square. The Egyptians also knew how to calculate the areas of triangles and circles. The latter was important for working out quantities of grain in cylindrical vessels. This required an understanding of pi, which was calculated as 3.16 instead of 3.142.

The unit of weight was the deben, equivalent to 3.29 ounces. Later the kite was introduced and the system was rationalized so that 10 kite = 1 deben. Although Egypt was a nonmonetary economy, goods were given a notional value in deben of copper, silver, or gold, thus allowing transactions to take place more easily.

Capacity was measured in *hin*—about one pint—ten of which made one *hektat*.

Opposite: Detail of a wall painting from the tomb of Panekhmen, depicting metalworkers weighing gold on scales. Wealthy individuals were buried with the fruits of their success in the mortal world, though sustenance was the prime consideration. This was meant to be provided by family and friends, but the suspicion was that this practice would be curtailed at some point. The magical properties of painted images or models of food deposited in the tomb would then be called upon.

Right: Relief fragment from a Nineteenth Dynasty tomb showing a carpenter at work using an adze. Everyday scenes of work and leisure were used to create a perfect mortal world, which would be recreated in the eternal life. The disheveled appearance of this worker is something of an aberration in tomb imagery.

Below: Limestone painting depicting a scene from a fable: a cat bearing a shepherd's crook guards a nest of geese and their eggs. Cats were valued both as domestic animals and for their association with the deities, notably Bastet and Re. During the Middle Kingdom cats regularly featured in the wall paintings of private tombs, often in hunting scenes with their master. By the New Kingdom the cat achieved apotheosis, and thereafter large numbers were mummified and buried in dedicated cemeteries, notably in Bubastis, the cult center of Bastet.

Above: Scene from the tomb of Userhet, royal scribe to Amenhotep II (c. 1427–c. 1400 BC). The upper register shows an officer addressing new recruits. In the middle register, some of the recruits are pictured having their hair cut. During the Dynastic period shaving became increasingly popular among the upper echelons of Egyptian society, and facial hair came to be seen as a mark of inferior status. However, beards were associated with the deities, and they featured in funerary images of both royal and nonroyal personages. The pharaoh was invariably depicted with a false beard, establishing his status as a living god, while the tombs of ordinary individuals often show the deceased with a short beard.

Overleaf: Detail of a wall painting from the tomb of Sennedjem at Deir el-Medina. The tomb owner and his wife are shown plowing the Field of Reeds, also known as the Field of Iaru. This is a symbolic image, and is not meant to imply that Sennedjem was involved in agricultural work during his lifetime. The field was the domain of Osiris, king of the Underworld, and passage through it was a metaphor for the transition between life and death.

Opposite: Detail of a wall painting from the tomb of Rekhmire, vizier to two Eighteenth Dynasty pharaohs, Tuthmosis III and Amenhotep II. The tomb scenes show a number of craftsmen working on state projects, the supervision of which would have come under Rekhmire's remit. This scene depicts the stages of the mudbrick-making process.

Towns and Housing

Egyptian towns were usually built on a grid system, with houses typically constructed in terraces. Town planning and social stratification were interlinked, as different areas housed important officials, craftworkers and laborers.

The basic building block was mudbrick. A mix of mud, straw, and stone was poured into molds and hardened in the sun. Fired bricks were introduced during the New Kingdom. Roofs were supported by palm logs, while floors were of packed earth, sometimes with papyrus matting.

Near the entrance to a home there was usually an image of Bes, a ferocious-looking dwarf god who was actually the benign protector of the family.

The houses of the more affluent were multistory, and sometimes raised off the ground to prevent damp penetration. These may also have had plastered and painted internal walls. The outer walls were whitewashed to reflect the heat, with small, north-facing windows built into them. This kept the interior at a comfortable temperature whatever the ambient conditions. However, it did mean there was little natural light, and oil-filled pottery lamps were used. Most homes were sparsely furnished. Beds, stools, tables, benches, and boxes were the most common pieces of furniture, and these were usually made of wood. Chairs were found only in the homes of the wealthy, and the furniture here was much more elegant and ornate.

There was no sanitation, although there is evidence that some houses did have bathrooms. Cooking was done by clay oven or open fire, fueled by charcoal or wood.

Above: Vignette from the Book of the Dead showing Nakht, an Eighteenth Dynasty scribe and astronomer, who together with his wife Tawi stands in judgment before Osiris, although the god is not shown. The brilliantly vivid scenes of Nakht at work and enjoying leisure activities make his tomb one of the finest in Thebes' Valley of the Nobles.

Right: Vignette from the Book of the Dead, showing the deceased and his wife at prayer. A spell is to be recited to the moon in its young phase, on the first day of the month. The Book of the Dead, introduced at the beginning of the New Kingdom, consisted of some 200 spells, many derived from the earlier Pyramid and Coffin Texts. Unlike the earlier funerary texts, which were the exclusive preserve of royalty and the wealthy, the Book of the Dead was available to anyone who could afford a papyrus copy. Some of the spells were presented in hieroglyphic text, or its cursive derivatives, while others were illustrated in the form of vignettes. The Book of the Dead was placed either inside the coffin or within the wrappings of the mummified body.

Opposite: In another vignette from the Book of the Dead, the deceased kneels before Anubis, god of mummification. As well as being recorded on papyrus, some spells were also inscribed on amulets or shabti figures that were placed in the tomb.

Papyrus

Papyrus grew abundantly in the delta region during the Pharaonic era and was the heraldic emblem of Lower Egypt. It translates as "pertaining to the king," suggesting that this important natural resource was regarded as crown property.

Papyrus had both symbolic significance and myriad practical applications. On a symbolic level it was the plant that flourished on the primeval mound of creation myths. All Egyptian temple sites symbolized the patch of land from which life sprang in the midst of watery chaos. The papyrus motif thus featured prominently in temple architecture, particularly in the columns of hypostyle halls.

On a practical level, the coarse outer layer of the papyrus stem was used for boat-building, basketry, ropes, matting, and sandals. To make sheets for writing purposes the pith was soaked, cut into thin strips, and placed in special formwork. A second layer was laid on top, at right-angles to the first. The papyrus was then beaten to release water and starch, which acted as a bonding agent. Weights were applied as the sheets dried.

Although individual pieces of papyrus did not exceed 20 inches in length they could be glued together to form a roll. The largest in existence is the Great Harris Papyrus, housed in the British Museum. This document, which chronicles the reign of Rameses III in hieratic script, is 134 ft long.

The use of papyrus as a writing material continued long after the Pharaonic era came to an end. It declined after the ninth century AD, when cloth paper was introduced in the Far East. The modern product is a wood-pulp derivative, yet the word "paper" takes its name from its Ancient Egyptian counterpart.

Opposite: Detail from a funerary text showing the sky goddess Nut spreading her wings over the deceased. As Nut was believed to swallow the sun each evening and give birth to it at dawn, she often featured in tomb imagery. Also shown is the jackal-headed Anubis, who was guardian of the necropolis as well as being god of mummification. Kneeling beneath Anubis are the sister goddesses Isis and Nephthys, who offered protection to the deceased and appeared in judgment scenes in the Book of the Dead.

Above: Eighteenth Dynasty mummy mask. As early as the Old Kingdom sculpted limestone heads were placed in the burial chamber, to become animate in the afterlife and also possibly to enable the returning spirit to identify its corporeal form. Masks evolved to fulfil the same purpose. At first a plaster mold was made from the features of the deceased. In the First Intermediate period cartonnage was used: strips of linen stiffened with plaster. By the New Kingdom the process reached its ultimate refinement with solid gold death masks similar to that found on the mummified Tutankhamun.

Craft and Technology

Artisans of all kinds were respected members of society, their skills highly valued and well rewarded. There was usually a sector of urban areas given over to craftworkers, and by the end of the Old Kingdom production tended to be a collaborative rather than individual process, an early form of mass production.

There were masons, carpenters, potters, jewelers, and metal, glass, and textiles workers. Some of their output was purely utilitarian but from the earliest times aesthetic beauty was prized.

Copper was the first metal to be exploited. By the Early Dynastic period copper-smelting was well developed, although bellows did not appear until the New Kingdom; before then reed pipes were used. Utensils, tools, and weapons were made, and examples of copper statuary dating from the Old Kingdom have been found. Bronze came from Asia

early in the Dynastic era but was not in widespread use until the Middle Kingdom.

Masons mainly worked with limestone, sandstone, and granite, although alabaster, basalt, quartzite, and greywacke were also used. The quality of woodwork improved markedly with the introduction of copper tools in the Early Dynastic period. The carpenter's toolkit typically comprised the axe, saw, adze, chisel, mallet, bradawl, and bow-drill. There were no planes; smoothing was done by adze and sandstone. Sophisticated techniques such as dovetailing, mitred corners and mortise-and-tenon joints were applied. Multilayer plywood was used during the Old Kingdom and veneered furniture appeared c. 1500 BC.

Pottery made from Nile silt was used for utilitarian goods, with marl clay from Quena reserved for pieces of superior quality. The potter's wheel was

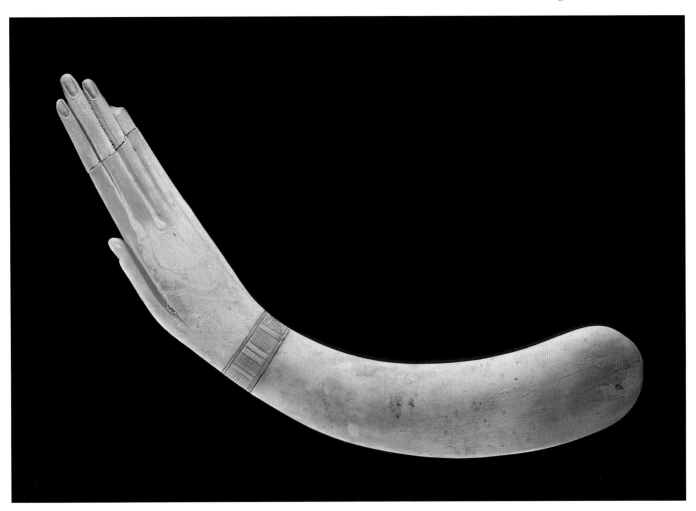

developed during the Fifth Dynasty, and the chimney kiln arrived at around the same time. The latter facilitated mass production, with temperatures up to 800 degrees centigrade being generated. However, glaze was not applied until the Roman era.

One of the most important ceramic materials was faience, made from crushed quartz or quartzite sand. Often coated with a green or blue glaze, faience was used throughout the Dynastic era to produce vessels, charms, figurines, and jewelry. It was a cheap alternative to precious stones such as lapis lazuli and turquoise, which it resembled. Later, colored glass was used to create the same effect. It was also set in gold to create high quality jewelry, a technique known as cloisonné. Glass was a luxury product, used for small containers such as cosmetics jars. Such vessels were made by core-forming. A mud-sand mold was used to

form the interior shape of the vessel, and this was then dipped into the molten glass. Glass-blowing did not arrive until the Ptolemaic period.

Jewelry was worn by both men and women and was not the preserve of the wealthy. Apart from its decorative purpose jewelry was also used to denote social status and, in amulet form, to provide protection. Rings, bracelets, necklaces, diadems, chokers, earrings, and anklets have all been identified, and the fact that jewelry featured prominently among funerary goods shows that Egyptians prized adornment no less in the afterlife. Jewelers worked with gold, silver, and a number of precious and semi-precious stones including turquoise, lapis lazuli, feldspar, amethyst, and cornelian. Gold was also inlaid into the best furniture, and in leaf form it was used to gild statues, coffins, and other grave goods.

Previous pages (left): Glass unguent or cosmetics jar, dating from the Amarna period of the Eighteenth Dynasty. Glass-making did not appear in Egypt until the Middle Kingdom. The earliest pieces were made from imported glass ingots or scrap material known as cullet. The technology to make glass from silica came much later, learned from craftsmen in other lands where it had already been developed. The transfer of skill was probably in the wake of either conquest or migration.

Previous pages (right): Ivory clapper in the form of a hand. Clappers, made from ivory, wood, or bone, were used to provide a rhythmic beat for both work and entertainment. This was Egypt's oldest musical instrument, dating from the Predynastic era. Clappers were part of a percussion instrument group known as idiophones which were particularly associated with religious rituals. Bells, cymbals, and the sistrum—a kind of rattle—were also in this group. Musicians performing before cult statues of the gods would not have been allowed to lay eyes on these sacred figures. Blind players were probably used for this purpose, a theory supported by many tomb paintings.

Left: Vulture-shaped collar. This bird's vast wingspan meant that it was associated with a protective rather than predatory quality.

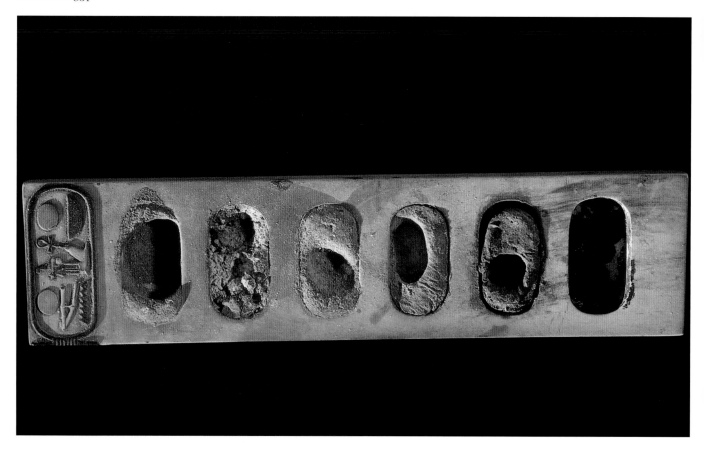

Above: Eighteenth Dynasty ivory palette containing six blocks of pigment. The cartouche indicates that it dates from the reign of Amenhotep III. Stone palettes for grinding pigment used as eyepaint date from the Predynastic period, and were used by both sexes. As well as for enhancing the appearance, eyepaint also protected the eyes from sand particles and the glare of the sun. There was also probably an element of religious symbolism.

Left: Block of wooden ointment containers, individually inscribed, dating from the Eighteenth Dynasty.

Opposite: Cosmetic spoon in the form of a young woman carrying an amphora on her shoulder. Items of cosmetic equipment and the jars into which the cosmetics were decanted were often highly embellished; form and function combined, just as in the modern beauty treatment industry. Cosmetics and mirrors also featured prominently among funerary goods, indicating that adornment was regarded as important in the afterlife.

Enhancing the Appearance

Adornment of the body was important to the Ancient Egyptians. Both men and women wore makeup, wigs, and scent, and there is also evidence for manicures and pedicures. Green malachite-based eyepaint was used during the Early Dynastic period. Kohl, a black eye-liner made from ground galena or soot, is still used today. Eye makeup enhanced the appearance but it also had a more practical purpose: the fatty substances offered protection against airborne sand particles; they were also thought to fight infection and even cure defective eyesight. There was face powder and lipstick made from red ochre; nail polish and henna was used for dyeing the hair. Perfumed cones of animal fat were attached to headgear or wigs, releasing their fragrant odor as they melted.

The better-off could beautify themselves in front of mirrors of burnished metal. These were often adorned with motifs of Hathor, goddess of love. The concept of love potions also existed; disgusting concoctions were taken in the hope of attracting a particular mate. There were even brand names such as "Elixir of Aphrodite" to give a product exotic appeal. Cosmetics were often included in funerary goods, suggesting that enhancing the appearance would be no less important in the afterlife.

Opposite: Eighteenth Dynasty sculpture depicting Isis suckling the infant Horus. It is made from Egyptian blue, a material akin to glass. The technique of glass-blowing did not arrive until the period of Roman occupation. Until then glassware was made either in moulds or by core-forming. The latter involved making a mold of the interior shape of a vessel, which was then dipped in molten glass or had the molten material poured over it.

Left: This ornate box, dating from the Eighteenth Dynasty, was used as a container for jars of cosmetics and fragrances.

Right: Ivory-paneled casket, dating from the reign of Rameses IX (c. 1126–c. 1108 BC). It was found at the Theban necropolis of Deir el-Bahri, one of many items moved there from the Valley of the Kings by Twenty-first Dynasty priests of Amun to protect them from the attention of grave-robbers. The cache included some forty royal mummies, among them Tuthmosis I, II and III and Rameses II, III, and IX. These were discovered by chance in 1871, after a villager went to the rescue of a goat which had fallen down a shaft. He realized he had stumbled across a treasure trove, and tried to sell the contents on the antiquities market. It was not until 1881 that French Egyptologist Gaston Maspero comprehensively excavated the site.

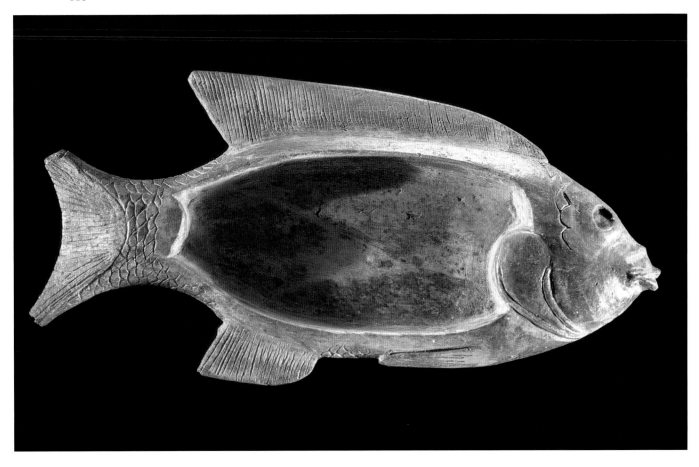

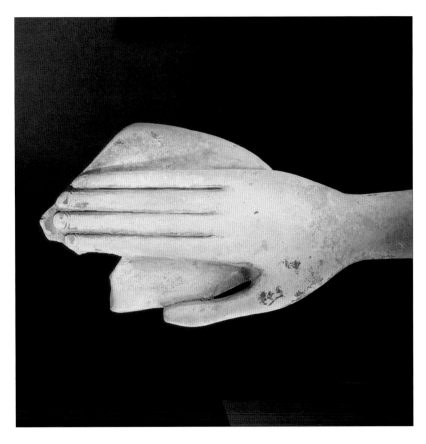

Above: Fish-shaped cosmetic dish, probably used for funerary anointing rituals. The Egyptians had ambivalent feelings regarding fish. Some were seen as sacred, for example the Nile perch, which was associated with the goddess Neith. There was also a connection with malevolence, Osiris's penis having been eaten by fish after the king's dismemberment by the evil Seth. The pharaohs and priesthood did not eat fish for this reason, although other strata of society ate fish as a cheap alternative to meat.

Left: Cosmetic spoon in the form of a hand holding a shell.

Opposite above: Gaming board and pieces to play either senet *or "twenty squares." The former was a very popular game, in which two players vied to move their pieces round the board. Moves were determined by the use of throwsticks, akin to the modern die. Certain squares represented good or i§ fortune, leading to speculation that when included in funerary equipment,* senet *assumed symbolic significance.*

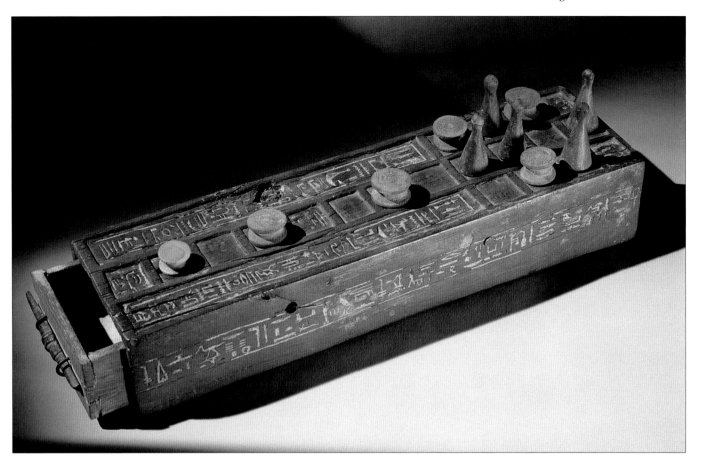

Sport and Pastimes

Muscularity and fitness were not necessarily regarded as positive attributes as they suggested physical toil, associated with the lower echelons of society. Of the eight corporal elements identified by the Egyptians, none was concerned with development of the physique. Indeed bodily girth, with the implication of being well fed and well heeled, was in itself a status symbol. This attitude may have changed over time, particularly during periods of military success where athleticism and battlefield prowess went hand-in-hand.

Archery, ship-handling, chariot-racing, and big-game-hunting were all incorporated into military training. Egyptians hunted for pleasure as well as food, fishing and fowling being the most popular pursuits. In the New Kingdom running, boxing, wrestling, and fencing were introduced into the army regime and these soon crossed over into civilian life. By the Twenty-fifth Dynasty long jump, high jump, and weightlifting were also common.

Sedentary pursuits included a number of board games, the most popular being *senet* and *mehen*. The former involved moving counters across a grid of thirty squares, some of which brought good fortune, others bad. Moves were determined by throwsticks, a forerunner to dice. *Mehen* was played on a circular board, each player having a number of ordinary counters and one lion counter. The winner was the player whose predatory piece devoured most of his opponent's counters. Gaming boards were often included in funerary goods to provide entertainment in the afterlife.

There were children's games such as leap-frog and a version of blind-man's-buff, and a wide range of toys including rattles, balls, spinning tops, skittles, dolls, and carved animals. As the use of dolls had wider symbolic resonance, assigning the term "toy" exclusively to a particular item is no straightforward task. Some objects were probably purely playthings, while others may have had a symbolic element too.

CHAPTER FIVE

Decline and Fall
c. 1069 BC–AD 641

Dynasties Twenty-one to Twenty-four, collectively known as the Third Intermediate period, saw Egypt experience instability, fragmentation, and invasion from both north and south. Smendes, founder of the Twenty-first Dynasty, established a new capital at Tanis in the delta region. But his rule did not extend to Thebes, where the High Priests of Amun continued to hold sway over large parts of the country. Eventually an accommodation was reached by which Thebans recognized Smendes as pharaoh, in return for which Tanis did not challenge the autonomy of Upper Egypt. Intermarriage between the two rival lines over time helped maintain this arrangement.

Sheshonq I

The last Twenty-first Dynasty king died without leaving a male heir, and the throne passed to his son-in-law, the army commander Sheshonq, who founded a new royal line. Sheshonq I was of Libyan descent but hailed from Bubastis in the eastern delta region. Although Tanis remained the political hub, housing the royal residence and necropolis, Bubastis became an important town during this period. It was also the cult center of the cat deity Bastet, daughter of the Sun God. Bastet was sometimes portrayed with the head of a lioness, suggesting ferocity, but in the Later Dynastic period she was mostly depicted in a protective role, as a domestic cat surrounded by kittens.

Opposite: Gold funerary mask of the Twenty-first Dynasty king Psusennes I. His was one of a number of tombs unearthed in 1939 at the delta town of Tanis, the necropolis for a number of rulers of the Third Intermediate period.

Under Sheshonq I trade flourished and Egypt's dominion over Palestine was restored after an attack on Jerusalem, the latter campaign recorded on the Bubastite Portal at the Temple of Amun at Karnak. These achievements did not bring greater unity. Tension between the delta rulers and Thebes increased, particularly regarding the imposition of a royal placeman as High Priest of Amun. There was civil strife as other centers, including Herakleopolis and the western delta town of Sais, vied for power with Tanis and Thebes. None seems to have gained overall control of the country. A Saite prince named Tefnakht came closest to uniting the land but he was confronted by a new threat, from the Kushite ruler Piy. Based at Napata, Piy had gained control of Nubia and now had expansionist designs on Egypt. A stela at the sacred mountain site of Gebel Barkal in Upper Nubia records Piy's advance northward and Tefnakht's capitulation. The victorious Piy returned to Nubia, leaving an occupying force to administer the conquered land. He installed his sister, Amendiris, as God's Wife of Amun. This powerful position, dating from the Twenty-first Dynasty, involved playing consort to Amun during religious ceremonies. It had been held by the king's daughter, thus reaffirming the link between the incumbent of the throne and the gods. As the God's Wife of Amun was required to remain a virgin, the post passed to the daughter of the next pharaoh. It was thus as much about political stability as religious observance, for the new king's power base at Thebes was guaranteed.

The Assyrians

Piy was succeeded by his brother Shabaqo. He too waged a successful military campaign in Egypt and,

Above: Glass fragment depicting two half-faces of the dwarf god Bes, whose grotesque appearance belied his benign role as protector of the family.

and a protracted struggle ensued between the Assyrians and successive Napatan kings. Esarhaddon installed the Saite prince Nekau as nominal ruler and he founded the Twenty-sixth Dynasty. The Napatan king Tanutamani, who came to the throne in 664 BC, launched a fresh assault on Egypt. He reached Memphis and Nekau was killed in battle. This success was shortlived as a year later the Assyrian leader Ashurbanipal struck back and drove Tanutamani back to Nubia. Nekau's son Psamtek was placed on the throne to continue the Saite line of the Twenty-sixth Dynasty, ruling from Memphis. The Assyrians withdrew and the threat from Nubia subsided.

Psamtek

Psamtek was probably little more than a puppet leader initially, but when the Assyrians themselves came under threat from Babylonia at home, Egypt was left to its own devices. Psamtek shrewdly consolidated his position in a number of ways. He installed his daughter Nitiqret as God's Wife of Amun, which established a vital foothold in Thebes. Mindful of regional power bases that had fragmented the country for so long, the king encouraged settlement. There was immigration on a large scale, by Carians, Jews, Syrians, and in particular by Greeks, who eventually had their own purpose-built city in the delta, Naucratis. The incomers naturally diluted any potential opposition to Psamtek's right to rule Egypt. Similarly, the fact that the Egyptian army included foreign mercenaries lessened the likelihood of dissent or a coup.

Perhaps in reaction to these demographic changes there was a brief revival of nationalistic pride. Egyptians looked to their traditional roots in art, architecture, literature, and religion, trying to recreate the skills, customs, and beliefs of a bygone era. It was but a fleeting attempt to recreate a glorious past; Egypt was soon in decline again.

Nekau II, Psamtek's son and successor, campaigned in Syria and Palestine, like so many Egyptian kings before him. He enjoyed success there but then faced the new dominant force in the Near East. Babylonia had supplanted Assyria as western Asia's greatest power, and in 605 BC Nebuchadnezzar defeated Nekau II's army in the Battle of Carchemish. Four years later Nebuchadnezzar, by now ruler of the Babylonian Empire, attempted to invade Egypt but this time the onslaught was successfully repulsed.

Nekau II's successor, Psamtek II, avoided conflict with

unlike his brother, consolidated his victory. Shabaqo gained control of Lower Egypt by defeating the Twenty-fourth Dynasty Saite king Bakenrenef, son of Tefnakht, and establishing a new regnal line.

Shabaqo proclaimed himself pharaoh, choosing Thebes as his capital. Like the indigenous population, the Napatans regarded Amun-Re as the pre-eminent deity, and under their rule many Egyptian traditions were observed. Even so the old regional power bases were never fully extinguished. However, Egypt's overlord soon had a much greater threat to contend with. Assyria was emerging as the dominant force in the Near East. When the Assyrians threatened Syria and Palestine, territories over which Egypt had had dominion, it brought the new and old imperial powers onto a collision course. In 701 BC Hezekiah, king of the besieged land of Palestine, sought help from Shabaqo's successor, Shabitqo. An army was dispatched and although it was defeated by the Assyrians, the latter did finally withdraw from Palestine. Over the following thirty years the friction between the two countries continued. In 671 BC Assyria, now ruled by Esarhaddon, mounted a second direct attack on Egypt, the first having been repulsed. This time Memphis was taken

Babylonia but had to confront more unrest in Nubia. This time the fragile loyalty of the mercenaries proved costly as soldiers of the border garrison deserted in droves over conditions of service. Psamtek II led his forces into Nubia and quelled the incipient uprising.

The following Egyptian king, Apries, was drawn into further hostilities with Babylonia. An Egyptian army intervened as Palestine again came under attack, this time in the form of King Nebuchadnezzar. Egypt couldn't prevent the fall of Jerusalem but many Jews who avoided being taken into captivity were given refuge on the island of Elephantine.

Ahmose II

In 570 BC Apries intervened in another foreign dispute, one which precipitated his downfall. Libya was uneasy about a Greek colony that had been established on the north African coast and requested military assistance from Egypt to mount an offensive. The Egyptian army was routed, Apries' reputation dealt a mortal blow. The king was subsequently ousted in a military coup, a general named Amasis taking the throne and enjoying widespread support. Apries was imprisoned, and it appears was later killed after being handed over to a mob. Amasis, who ruled as Ahmose II, accorded his predecessor a funeral befitting a pharaoh. This helped to legitimize and consolidate his own position, an example of the shrewdness that would be one of the hallmarks of the popular new king. Another characteristic was a weakness for drink, but even so under Ahmose II Egypt enjoyed a thirty-year period of peace and prosperity.

Ahmose remained wary of the Greek mercenaries who made a significant contribution to the strength of the Egyptian army. They had fought alongside Apries in the coup, and Ahmose now curbed that country's influence in Egypt by limiting its ability to trade; Greek merchants could now operate only in the delta city of Naucratis.

Persia

In 526 BC Ahmose was succeeded by his son, Psamtek III, whose reign was brought to an end within a matter of months by a bellicose new imperial power. Persia, under Cyrus II, had already annexed large swathes of the Near East, including Syria, Palestine, and Babylon. Cyrus II's son, Cambyses, inherited his father's expansionist designs along with the throne, and in 525 BC turned his eyes on

Left: Decorative hieroglyphs of the Book of the Dead, from the coffin of Petosiris, High Priest of Thoth in the early Ptolemaic period. The Book of the Dead consisted of some 200 spells whose function was to assist the deceased on his passage to the afterlife.

Egypt. Psamtek III's army was defeated at the Battle of Pelusium, Memphis was taken, and the king himself was subsequently executed. Cambyses was proclaimed pharaoh and founder of the Twenty-seventh Dynasty, the beginning of a 120-year period of Persian rule. The six kings who reigned during this period largely saw Egypt as an outpost of the Persian Empire and delegated the running of the country to appointed governors. These regimes were generally harsh, although some Persian kings did make an effort to respect Egyptian traditions and beliefs. The dynasty's second ruler, Darius I, was the most enlightened in this regard, building temples to Amun-Re at Hibis and Qasr el-Ghueida, undertaking civil engineering projects and instructing that Egyptian law be codified. Under Darius's rule, 522 BC–486 BC, Egypt enjoyed a period of stability, and Egyptians were coopted to work and fight for Persia in other parts of her empire. However, Persia's defeat by Greece at the Battle of Marathon in 490 BC appears to have stirred rebellious thoughts and galvanized the Egyptians into action. In 486 BC Darius I was succeeded by Xerxes, and one of his first tasks was to quell an attempted uprising. Xerxes had none

of the liberal inclinations of his predecessor, and relations between the indigenous population and the imperial overlord worsened during his twenty-one-year reign. After his death in 465 BC the new ruler, Artaxerxes I, faced a fresh insurrection in the delta region. Although the Egyptians received Athenian backing in the enterprise, they failed in their attempt to take Memphis, and Persia retained its grip on the country.

For the remainder of Artaxerxes I's reign and that of his successor, Darius II, resentment simmered but there was no major rebellion. In 404 BC, the year following Darius II's death, Egypt finally wrested control of the country from Persia. A Saite prince named Amyrtaios seized power, helped by the fact that Persia's resources were thinly stretched during a troubled period for the empire. Amyrtaios founded the Twenty-eighth Dynasty, and over the next four years the expulsion of the Persians from Egypt was completed. Amyrtaios himself died shortly afterward, and with his demise the shortest dynasty in Egypt's history came to an end.

The Thirtieth Dynasty

Amyrtaios' legacy was a country once again united and independent. The inheritors were princes from the delta city of Mendes, although it is not clear whether the first

Below: Glass fragments from the Greco-Roman period, when glass-blowing was introduced. These pieces were found in Alexandria, the chief center for glass craftsmanship during this time.

king of this new line, Nepherites I, toppled Amyrtaios and usurped the throne. Persia sought to reconquer her former territory but in the short term the reconstituted Egyptian army, once again with the assistance of mercenaries, withstood the challenge.

Around 380 BC the throne passed to a new line, which hailed from another delta city, Sebennytos. The three kings of this, the Thirtieth Dynasty, presided for some forty years over a country that once again sought to capture the glories of Egypt's proud heritage. In particular this manifested itself in the construction of some spectacular monuments, and an even keener enthusiasm for traditional cult worship.

By 343 BC Egypt was again economically strong and had secured its borders for sixty years. Nectanebo II had become the Thirtieth Dynasty's third king, seizing power seventeen years earlier from his uncle, Teos. But he was destined to be the last Egyptian-born pharaoh, for in 343 BC a 300,000-strong Persian army, led by Artaxerxes III, mounted a successful invasion. Nectanebo was forced to retreat to Upper Egypt, but even this was but a temporary respite for soon the whole of Egypt fell under Persian control. There was looting and destruction on a widespread scale before Artaxerxes installed a satrap or governor and departed the country, taking with him sacred works of literature and statues of Egypt's deities. Nectanebo's fate is unknown.

Above: Late period bronze figure of a cat, a sacred animal chiefly associated with the goddess Bastet. Many mummified cats have been found at Bubastis, the delta town which was Bastet's cult center.

Alexander the Great

The Second Persian period—the Thirty-first Dynasty—lasted barely a decade. In 332 BC Egypt found itself with a new imperial overlord as Alexander the Great of Macedonia brought an end not only to Persia's control of that country but to her period as the dominant power in the Mediterranean and Near East. Alexander the Great seems to have met little resistance in displacing the Persians and establishing Greece's authority in Egypt. An oracle declared him son of Amun-Re, which gave legitimacy to his claim to the throne. He showed respect for Egypt's traditions and customs, and engaged in sacrificial rituals to Egyptian gods, which to the indigenous population would have marked the new

regime out from the hated Persian oppressors. The events of 332 BC were seen as more an act of liberation than invasion, and Alexander was duly proclaimed pharaoh. Thus began three centuries of Macedonian rule, known as the Ptolemaic period.

Alexander the Great was soon on the conquest trail again, but remained in Egypt long enough to found the city of Alexandria, on the western side of the country's Mediterranean coast. The Macedonian ruler had established new cities in other conquered lands, regarding it as a means of disseminating Greek culture. Another means of assimilating a subjugated people was by the introduction of coinage bearing his image and promoting trade both throughout the empire and beyond it. In short, Alexander the Great sought to promote commonality within the empire but also to appreciate and tolerate difference. He was well aware that the stick might allow Macedonia to gain control of a country but the carrot was important to make the conquest more easily sustainable.

Alexandria soon replaced Memphis as the country's capital and would remain a thriving cosmopolitan city throughout the Greco-Roman period. It became renowned as a seat of learning, home to the Great Library and Museum, built during the reign of Ptolemy I. There was also the lighthouse on the island of Pharos, usually included in the Seven Wonders of the Ancient World. Neither survived to the modern era: the Library and Museum were destroyed by fire in the third century AD, the lighthouse by an earthquake in the fourteenth century.

The Ptolemies

Following Alexander's departure after only some six months in Egypt, the country was administered by a viceroy and several governors. On Alexander the Great's sudden death in 323 BC the crown passed to his half-brother, Philip Arrhidaeus, and son, Alexander IV. Even during the eighteen-year period in which these two reigned, the Macedonian Empire was administered largely through generals, whose number included Ptolemy. Following the death of Alexander IV, the last

Below: Vignette from the Book of the Dead, showing the deceased engaged in agricultural work in the Field of Reeds. Crops grew in abundance in this imaginary field, passage through which was a metaphor for the journey to the afterlife.

natural heir in the line, the division of the empire was formalized. In 305 BC Ptolemy proclaimed himself king of Egypt, ruling as Ptolemy I Soter, the appended epithet meaning "savior". It was the beginning of a 275-year period of Hellenistic rule, fourteen subsequent kings of the same name sitting on the Egyptian throne.

Greek was now the official language of the country. A Greco-Egyptian culture emerged in the delta region, and produced an artistic style which represented a departure from that of the Dynastic era. By contrast the architecture of Upper Egypt remained impervious to Greek, and later Roman, influences.

Securing the line of succession was the primary consideration of the Ptolemies. The practice of appointing the son and heir to the throne as coregent was adopted, the tradition of royal brother-sister marriages reintroduced. Ptolemy II elevated his wife and sister, Arsinoe II, to the ranks of the deities, a practice which successive kings followed. Not only was there religious tolerance, the Ptolemies also built great temples to Egyptian gods, for example at Edfu and Dendera, cult centers of Horus and Hathor respectively. Ptolemy I also introduced the syncretic god Serapis, who was a concatenation of Osiris and several Greek gods, including Zeus.

In general the actions of the Ptolemies—even those which seemed enlightened and benevolent—were motivated by a desire to maintain order and control. They did not embrace Egyptian culture and were indifferent to its traditions. Taxes were punitive and the kings were quick to exploit Egypt's rich resources. The country was

wealthy but the chief beneficiaries of the prosperity were the ruling elite, not the native population. Such attitudes and practices bred resentment, within the Egyptian-born ranks of the army as well as the general population, and there were a number of uprisings. In 206 BC, during the reign of Ptolemy IV, one such rebellion resulted in the establishment of an enclave in Upper Egypt where the native population enjoyed a degree of autonomy, under a ruler named Horwennefer. This independent state existed for almost two decades before being suppressed by the next king, Ptolemy V Epiphanes.

Ptolemy V was four years old when he acceded to the throne. Ten years later he was accorded two coronation ceremonies, one according to Macedonian custom, one following Egyptian convention. This was part of a deliberate policy aimed at reasserting Greece's authority and subduing unrest. A decree, issued on March 27, 196 BC, commemorated the coronation and installation of the boy-king as a god in all temples. It was recorded on a slab of basalt in two Egyptian scripts, hieroglyphic and demotic, as well as Greek. The decree also granted privileges to the priesthood; the Ptolemies, like other kings before them, recognized that winning over the senior figures of the religious establishment was instrumental in maintaining royal authority. The discovery of a fragment of this slab, which became known as the Rosetta Stone, enabled Jean-François Champollion to break the hieroglyphic code 2000 years later.

In addition to unrest among the native population, the Ptolemies also faced losses of a sizeable amount of territory in other parts of the empire. If this wasn't enough the ruling dynasty was blighted from within, debauchery and degenerate behavior being a familiar characteristic during successive reigns. And in the second century BC the royal line fell victim to bloody, internecine warfare.

Euergetes II

In 180 BC Ptolemy V was poisoned by his wife, Cleopatra, the first of seven Egyptian queens who would bear that name. She ruled as regent before endorsing her son, Ptolemy Philometor, as the next king. This arrangement was strengthened when Philometor married his sister, also called Cleopatra. But a second son, Ptolemy Euergetes II, also had designs on power, and when Egypt was invaded by Syria and Philometor was captured, Alexandria proclaimed Euergetes II king. Syria withdrew, leaving Philometor to oversee Upper Egypt, while Euergetes II presided over Lower Egypt from his Alexandrian base. There was an uneasy peace as the

brothers vied for supremacy in the divided land. The economy also suffered in a country infected by intrigue and suspicion.

Matters improved temporarily when Rome, the great rising power, responded to a request to act as arbitrator in the dispute. Her decision left Philometor and Cleopatra to rule over Egypt, Euergetes II being awarded Cyrenaica.

Right: Gilt wooden statue of Osiris, king of the Underworld and god of resurrection and fertility.

But when Philometor died in 145 BC and bequeathed the throne to his son, Ptolemy VII Neos, Euergetes saw his chance. He married his brother's widow, the latter probably seeing this as the best way of retaining her own hands on power and securing her son's position. If so she was mistaken, for before the year was out Euergetes had murdered his nephew, having first insured the Egyptian throne would carry his own bloodline by making Cleopatra pregnant. He then took Cleopatra's daughter—his niece—for a wife. Cleopatra III, who was as ambitious as her mother, bore Euergetes five children and for years this triumvirate of convoluted familial relationships shared power.

There was still widespread discontent in the population at large, hardly tempered by the brutality and political chicanery that was going on at the seat of government. Euergetes, backed by a loyal mercenary army, meted out summary and savage treatment to any act of insurrection. Even so, the prevailing mood in the country finally became so hostile that the king temporarily abdicated with his wife-niece Cleopatra III and their children, together with his son by Cleopatra II. The latter was left in sole control of Egypt, but when she claimed the throne Euergetes responded by sending her the dismembered body of their son. He later returned to regain the Egyptian throne, and until his death in 116 BC the political status quo was restored, Euergetes and his mother-daughter wives sharing power.

The next generation saw more fraternal tension as the sons of Euergetes and Cleopatra III vied for the throne. Ptolemy IX Soter II was the anointed successor, but nine

years into his reign he was forced to share power with his younger brother, Ptolemy X Alexander. It was only after Alexander's death in 88 BC that the elder brother was able to enjoy eight more years in sole authority.

Cleopatra

Rome's increasing influence in Egypt's affairs again became apparent when she endorsed Ptolemy XI Alexander II—son of Ptolemy X—as the rightful inheritor of the throne on the death of Soter II in 80 BC. The new king was murdered three weeks later by an Alexandrian mob, and the throne passed to Ptolemy XII Neos, an illegitimate son of Soter II. During his twenty-

Right: A detail of a vignette from the Book of the Dead of Lady Cheritwebeshet showing a purification scene.

Opposite: Upper part of an anthropomorphic coffin, dating from the beginning of the Late Period, with blackened face, lotus ornamented wig, chest ornaments, and a picture of the deceased kneeling to offer flowers to Osiris.

nine-year reign Ptolemy XII increasingly deferred to Rome. On his death in 51 BC the throne passed to his daughter, Cleopatra VII, the most famous of the Egyptian queens of that name. A skilled political operator and clever opportunist, Cleopatra was the only ruler of the Ptolemaic period who troubled to learn the language of Greece's vassal state. She married in turn both her younger brothers, Ptolemy XIII and XIV, to consolidate her position. Her joint rule with Ptolemy XIII was a shortlived affair as she was ousted and forced to leave the country. Her fortunes changed with the arrival of Julius Caesar on the scene. Caesar had confirmed his position as dictator of Rome by defeating Pompey in battle in 47 BC. Pompey fled to Egypt, where he was killed by members of the royal court. Caesar followed, and Cleopatra petitioned him to restore her to power. No sooner was this done than Ptolemy XIII was drowned, and Cleopatra married her surviving brother, who ruled alongside her as Ptolemy XIV from 47 to 44 BC. She also became Caesar's lover and bore him a child. Cleopatra returned to Rome with Caesar, but after the latter's death in 44 BC she returned to Egypt, where her second husband was still in power. Ptolemy XIV died shortly afterwards in suspicious circumstances, leading some scholars to believe that Cleopatra was implicated in his death.

From 36 BC Cleopatra ruled Egypt with her son by Caesar, Ptolemy XV Caesarion, as coregent. By then she had turned her political and romantic eye on Mark Antony, a Roman consul who had been a member of the triumvirate that had shared power following Caesar's death. Antony sought leverage in his ongoing struggle with fellow triumvir Octavian, and the match with Cleopatra had a political dimension on his side also. Even so, it appears to have been a grand passion.

Antony and Cleopatra married in 40 BC and had three children. They also harbored thoughts of ruling jointly over the entire Roman Empire. Antony's enemies in Rome were monitoring the situation closely, particularly Octavian. Antony was married to his sister, Octavia; the animosity between the two thus had a private as well as a polical dimension. Antony was the victim of a propaganda campaign, denounced for the hedonistic lifestyle he was leading in Egypt and branded a traitor. In 31 BC Antony's forces met those of Octavian at sea, off the Greek coast at Actium. Antony was defeated and committed suicide on his return to Egypt. The triumphant Octavian arrived at Alexandria to claim the spoils of victory. Thirty-eight-year-old Cleopatra was not prepared to countenance the humiliation of being paraded in Rome. Legend has it that she too committed suicide, succumbing to the bite of a venomous snake on August 12, 30 BC.

Octavian, who would take the name Augustus and become the first Roman emperor, ordered the death of Ptolemy XV Caesarion to forestall the possibility of a future challenge from the son of Cleopatra and Julius Caesar. On August 31, 30 BC, he was proclaimed pharaoh and Egypt was formally subsumed within the Roman Empire.

The Greco-Roman Period

For 300 years Egypt was deemed a mere outpost of the Roman Empire, a vehicle for producing vital resources, particularly grain. Octavian and his successors may have adopted the title "pharaoh," but the course was set which would sever all links with Egypt's glorious past. Greek remained the official language, and Roman law was introduced. The cultural transformation was completed with the introduction of a new religion. Christianity arrived in Egypt in the first century AD and its tenets struck a favorable chord with many Egyptians. At first adherents of the new faith were persecuted by successive Roman emperors, notably Diocletian. In the fourth century AD Constantine I became the first emperor to endorse Christianity, resulting in the entire empire being converted in AD 324. Subsequently many great monuments and temples to the old deities were condemned as pagan and shut down or destroyed. This process was completed in AD 536 with the closure of the Temple of Isis at Philae.

The Greco-Roman period came to an end when Egypt was conquered by Arabs in AD 641. The country converted to Islam, although pockets of Christianity survived, the seeds of the Coptic Church which continues to flourish to this day, albeit as a minority. Egypt was later invaded by the Turks, and it was not until the 1960s that the country was once again led by a native Egyptian.

The end of Egypt's state religion was naturally reflected in art and architecture, which were informed by Christianity, and later, Islam. Cult worship—of the god-kings as well as the deities—cultural expression, and language were the hallmarks of the Pharaonic era. All were thus supplanted and a magnificent civilization came to an end, its glories and treasures waiting to be revisited and rediscovered by future generations.

Opposite: This sculpted head from the Ptolemaic period (332 BC–30 BC) is of an unidentified woman and known simply as La Dame d'Alexandrie.

Above left: Gold bangle mounted with lapis lazuli scarab, recovered from the tomb of the Twenty-second Dynasty ruler Sheshonq II. His hawk headed silver coffin was found in the tomb complex of an earlier king, Psusennes I, at Tanis in 1939. The treasures recovered from the delta necropolis are regarded as second only to those of Tutankhamun.

Above: Gold bracelet from the tomb of Amenemope, successor to the Twenty-first Dynasty king Psusennes I. The lapis lazuli scarab bears aloft the golden orb of the sun, symbol of resurrection through the association with the creator god Khepri. The artifacts recovered from Tanis are the most important source of information regarding funerary goods of the Third Intermediate period.

Left: Gold pectoral from the tomb of Amenemope, showing the king offering incense to the enthroned Osiris. The base is adorned with a row of djed *pillars, each consisting of two uprights with four crossbars. Regarded as Osiris's backbone, the djed pillar was sometimes shown with protruding arms holding symbols of kingship, the* ankh, crook, *and* flail. *A ceremony known as Raising the Djed Pillar was incorporated into the* heb sed *festival, when the reigning king's authority and virility were renewed. The pillar stood for the stability and longevity of the king of the Underworld, which the earthly ruler hoped to emulate.*

Right: Pectoral from the tomb of Psusennes I, made from gold, carnelian, lapis lazuli, and feldspar. It depicts a winged scarab flanked by kneeling figures of the sister-goddesses Isis and Nephthys. As mother of Horus, Isis was also regarded as the divine mother of the reigning king. Nephthys was not tainted by her role as wife to the evil Seth, murderer of Osiris. She helped Isis recover the dismembered body parts of her husband, and both goddesses assumed the role of protector of the dead. They were sometimes depicted as kites, the bird into which Isis transformed herself in an effort to breathe new life into Osiris. Nephthys was usually shown at the northern end of the royal sarcophagus, the direction in which the head of the deceased was orientated. Isis looked on from the southern aspect, aligned with the foot of the coffin.

Right: Coffin detail showing the sky goddess Nut, whose outstretched wings offer the deceased protection. As Nut was thought to swallow the setting sun and give birth to it each dawn, she was naturally an important funerary deity. Nut's body—in either human or bovine form—was thought to arch over the earth, her limbs indicating the cardinal compass points. It was a rift between Nut and the Sun God that was used by the Egyptians to account for the five extra days required to bring the 360-day Egyptian calendar in line with the solar year. Prevented from giving birth on any day of the Egyptian year, Nut was able to circumvent the ruling with the help of the moon god Thoth, who added five days to the calendar. Known as epagomenal days, these were said to have been when the five children of Nut and Geb were born. They were believed to be unlucky by the superstitious Egyptians, particularly the day on which the evil Seth was born.

Overleaf: Coffin detail showing Osiris, god of resurrection. Also depicted is the Wadjet eye, an important symbol of regeneration. Horus was said to have had his eyes put out by the evil Seth, but his sight was restored by Hathor. The Wadjet—or "healed"— eye often featured prominently in funeral iconography, the Egyptians believing its curative powers would help revivify the deceased in the afterlife.

Right: This pair of funerary sandals, made from sheet gold, was found on the mummified body of the Twenty-second Dynasty king Shoshenq II. They were discovered in 1939 by French Egyptologist Pierre Montet at the delta city of Tanis.

Psusennes II, the last Tanite ruler of this dynasty, died without heir. The throne passed to his son-in-law, the army commander Sheshonq, who came from the delta town of Bubastis but was of Libyan descent. As Sheshonq I he installed one of his sons as High Priest of Amun. This helped to restore a measure of royal control over Thebes but relations remained uneasy.

Above: Set of finger stalls, which preserved the fingers of the mummified royal body until they were restored in the afterlife.

Above: Fluted gold bowl, inset with faience, recovered from the tomb of one of the senior officials to the Third Intermediate period king Psusennes I. During the Twenty-second and Twenty-third Dynasties, c. 945 BC–c. 715 BC, several factions vied for control of Egypt. In addition to the Bubastite line descended from Sheshonq I and the Karnak priesthood at Thebes, rulers also emerged at Herakleopolis and Sais. None succeeded in gaining overall control and there were numerous concurrent reigns. There was also an external threat, from the Kushite leader Piy. He became the first Nubian leader to mount a successful conquest of Egypt. His son, Shabaqo, consolidated his father's victory and established a new royal line. The founding of this, the Twenty-fifth Dynasty, is regarded as the beginning of the Late period, when Egypt increasingly fell victim to hostile invaders.

Above: Detail from the coffin of Nespawershepi, Twenty-first Dynasty Chief of Scribes at the Temple of Amun, Karnak. Rain falls from the sky goddess Nut, bringing forth seedlings from the mummified body of Osiris, symbolizing the latter's regenerative powers. When Egypt fell under Kushite control, c. 747 BC, the Nubian rulers, beginning with Shabaqo, took the title of pharaoh and chose Thebes as their capital. They too regarded Amun-Re as the pre-eminent deity, and thus there was no great theological divide between Egypt's conquerors and the indigenous population. Even so, the country's regional power bases were never extinguished, and during the last centuries of the Dynastic era the Egyptians would struggle repeatedly to re-establish their autonomy.

Above: Another detail from Nespawershepi's coffin, showing the solar barque containing an image of the falcon-headed Re, who holds the ankh *sign. The Sun God is flanked by two baboons, sacred animals particularly associated with the moon deity Thoth.*

During the Twenty-fifth Dynasty Egypt's overlord, Nubia, came under increasing threat from the Assyrians, who in 671 BC mounted a successful invasion and captured Memphis. The Egyptian king Taharqo was driven southward, leaving the victorious Assyrian leader, Esarhaddon, to install native placemen to govern the country. One of this number was Nekau, a prince of the delta town of Sais, who became the founding ruler of the Twenty-sixth Dynasty. Nekau I was killed following a renewed attack by the Nubians, who in turn were routed by the returning Assyrians, led by the great warrior-king Ashurbanipal. The Saite line was restored, in the shape of Psamtek, son of Nekau, and the Nubian threat finally subsided.

Opposite: This Late period mummiform coffin shows a simplicity of style reminiscent of an earlier age. This accords with a national mood for recapturing past traditions in art, architecture, and literature, a mood born from demographic changes that occurred during this period. Under the Twenty-sixth Dynasty king Psamtek I there was largescale immigration into the country, a deliberate policy aimed at diluting any potential threat to his position by disaffected groups in the old regional power bases. Carians, Jews, and Syrians settled in Egypt, and in particular Greeks, who eventually had their own enclave in the delta, Naucratis. This policy was particularly important to the reigning king, since the Assyrian overlords who had put him in power were themselves under threat from the Babylonian Empire and could therefore offer Psamtek no support against internal insurgents.

Above: Twenty-sixth Dynasty relief showing servant women pressing oil from lilies for use in the manufacture of perfume. Egypt's efforts to revive the creative spirit of a glorious past quickly petered out. The country went into its final period of decline, hastened by a successful invasion mounted by the Persians in 525 BC. This marked the beginning of a 120-year period of Persian rule, during which the native population was subjected to harsh treatment.

Right: The Temple at Dendera, where Hathor, goddess of love, joy, and beauty, was worshiped. The Upper Egyptian town of Dendera was the chief cult center of Hathor for the entire Dynastic era. The buildings which survive today date from the reign of the Thirtieth Dynasty king Nectanebo I, with additions made during the Ptolemaic period. Pictured is the earliest surviving building, a mammisi or birth-house. These were appended to temple complexes from the Late period through to Roman times, and contained scenes celebrating divine births. In Hathor's case the child-god was Ihy, her son by Horus of Edfu. However, as the king was regarded as the living Horus, the mammisi would also have served to celebrate royal births. Indeed, it is known that plays describing the birth of both Ihy and the pharaoh were staged at Dendera, and it seems likely that dramatic reconstructions of this kind were a feature of all mammisi.

Above: Relief from the Temple of Horus at Edfu. It shows the falcon-headed god and his consort, Hathor, offering protection to two unidentified pharaohs. One of the kings wears the Red Crown of Upper Egypt, the other the Double Crown of the Two Lands. Horus himself is portrayed wearing the Double Crown, which he gained after emerging victorious from his long struggle with Seth. Scenes relating to their protracted battle for the Egyptian throne are recorded on the temple walls. The Temple at Edfu was constructed during the Ptolemaic period but is based on buildings dating back to the Old Kingdom.

Opposite: Relief from the barque shrine of Philip Arrhidaeus at Karnak, showing the fertility god Min. Egypt's long struggle against oppressive Persian rule was finally ended in 332 BC. Over the previous two centuries there had been a number of insurrections, and the Persians were driven from Egypt's shores for some sixty years. But a powerful army under Artaxerxes III returned in 343 BC and wrested control of Egypt once again. Eleven years later Alexander the Great of Macedonia expelled the hated Persians, a victory that was greeted as an act of liberation by the Egyptians. Following Alexander's death in 323 BC, control of the Macedonian Empire passed to his half-brother, Philip Arrhidaeus, and son Alexander IV. In practice, rule of Egypt was administered by army generals. When Alexander IV died in 305 BC, one of the governor-generals, Ptolemy of Lagos, became pharaoh. His descendants, all of the same name, ruled Egypt for the next 275 years.

The Temple at Philae, the main cult center of Isis, seen from the Nile. Situated five miles south of Aswan, the island of Philae symbolized the primeval mound of creation mythology. The oldest buildings date from the Late Dynastic era, but most of the temple complex was constructed during the Ptolemaic and Roman periods. It remained an important site in this time, since both Greek and Roman rulers adopted Egypt's traditions regarding royal lineage, seeing themselves as the living Horus, son of Isis. The cult of this popular goddess endured long after the introduction of Christianity. It was the last temple to be abandoned, an event which occurred during the reign of the Roman emperor Justinian in AD 536.

The construction of the Aswan Dam in the 1960s, which brought to an end the annual inundation cycle, flooded a vast area. The Temple of Philae would have been submerged beneath the newly formed Lake Nasser. An international effort, under the auspices of UNESCO, saw the temple, which also houses the last known hieroglyphic inscription, dismantled and rebuilt on the nearby island of Agilkia.

Cleopatra

The last ruler of the Ptolemaic line was Egypt's most famous queen, Cleopatra VII. Despite the mythology that grew to surround her, Cleopatra does not appear to have been a ravishing beauty. She was certainly politically astute and intellectually gifted, skills she employed to the maximum to secure power for herself and her children, an attempt which ended in failure and suicide.

Cleopatra ruled as co-regent with her father, Ptolemy XII, and thereafter with her brother, Ptolemy XIII, whom she also married. Ousted from power by Ptolemy XIII in 48 BC, Cleopatra temporarily removed to Syria. When the Roman consul Pompey fled to Egypt following defeat by Julius Caesar in the Battle of Pharsalia, Cleopatra used the situation to her advantage. Pompey had been appointed her guardian in the wake of her father's death. Following his assassination by members of the Egyptian court, Cleopatra appealed to the victorious Caesar, who had pursued Pompey to Egypt. Caesar restored her to the throne, and when Ptolemy XIII was drowned in the Nile during a skirmish with Roman soldiers, Cleopatra ruled alongside her second brother, Ptolemy XIV, whom she also married.

Cleopatra and Caesar—some thirty years her senior—became lovers, and a year later, 47 BC, she bore him a child, Ptolemy Caesarion. She accompanied Caesar to Rome in 46 BC, returning to Egypt after his assassination two years later. Ptolemy XIV was killed shortly afterwards, with Cleopatra widely believed to have been implicated. His death allowed Cleopatra and her son to become joint rulers of Egypt.

Cleopatra's next attempt to unite love and power came when she met Mark Antony, one of the triumvirate who ruled the Roman Empire after Caesar's death. Both were hugely ambitious and both sought political gain from the relationship, although it does appear to have been a grand passion. They married in 40 BC and Cleopatra bore Antony three children. In 34 BC, at a ceremony known as the Donations of Alexandria, Antony ceded parts of the empire to Cleopatra and her children. This antagonized Rome, not least Octavian, who was both political rival and embittered brother-in-law to Antony. He led a propaganda campaign, denouncing Antony as a hedonist and traitor. In 31 BC Octavian's fleet defeated Antony's forces at the Battle of Actium, Cleopatra's ships crucially withdrawing at the height of the engagement. The vanquished pair chose suicide over the ignominy of being paraded before their Roman victors. Legend has it that Cleopatra put a venomous snake to her breast on August 12, 30 BC. Octavian, who became the Roman Emperor Augustus, had Ptolemy Caesarion killed but spared Cleopatra's other children.

Opposite: One of many reliefs from the Temple of Horus at Edfu depicting the conflict between Horus and Seth. In these scenes Horus accompanies Re in his journey through the skies and wards off repeated attacks by the evil Seth. The triumph of the legitimate heir over the usurper was as important during the Hellenistic period as it was throughout the Dynastic era, borne out by the fact that the Temple at Edfu was constructed under the Ptolemies. When Egypt became Christianized, images of the traditional pantheon were seen as pagan and defaced, as can be seen here.

Top right: Fragment of a relief believed to a portrait of Cleopatra VII, the most famous of the Egyptian queens to bear that name. The last ruler of the Ptolemaic line, Cleopatra was clever, ruthless, and politically astute, though almost certainly not the alluring beauty of popular myth. Even so, she failed in her bid to prevent Egypt from becoming a vassal state of the Roman Empire in 30 BC.

Right: Head of Hathor wearing a beaded collar. This multifaceted goddess, depicted typically with flattened countenance and bovine ears, was the only deity to be portrayed full-face in reliefs. She appeared in this form in column capitals at the many temples and shrines dedicated to her.

Right: Spells from the Book of the Dead, here in hieroglyphic form, although the text was also sometimes reproduced in demotic and hieratic script. They were inscribed on the coffin of Petosiris, chief priest of the moon god Thoth during the reign of Ptolemy I, c. 300 BC. The burial chambers of Petosiris and his family are the most important private tombs at Tuna el-Gebel, the necropolis situated near Hermopolis Magna in Middle Egypt. The latter was the cult center of Thoth, who was also associated with knowledge and writing. A number of mummified baboons and ibises—animals both associated with Thoth—have been discovered at Tuna el-Gebel. However, the most interesting feature of this necropolis is the fusion of Egyptian and Hellenistic artistic styles in the tomb scenes. These show agricultural and craft workers and are of the kind consistent with the Egyptian tradition. On the other hand, the clothing and hairstyles are in a distinctive Greek style. This melding of artistic traditions was a rarity.

Left: Glass fragment depicting the falcon god Horus. During the Greco-Roman period various Egyptian deities were assimilated within the Hellenistic or Roman tradition. Thus, Horus might be shown wearing Roman armor, while Thoth was associated with Hermes, messenger and herald to the Greek gods. Similarly, Isis was linked to Demeter, the Greek fertility goddess, protector of women and marriage. The cult of Isis spread throughout Greece and to all parts of the Roman Empire. Temples dedicated to Isis were erected in Rome itself, her popularity rivaling both the Roman pantheon and Christianity.

Below: Glass Wadjet-eye plaque from the Greco-Roman period. Although such iconography was eventually discredited as paganism, the early Christianity of the Roman Empire was much influenced by Egyptian traditions. For example, images of Isis suckling Horus may well have been a theological template for the Madonna and Child.

Left: A gilt coffin dating from the Roman period, The Romans adopted many of the local customs on settling in Egypt. Some went as far as to follow Egyptian burial pratices, opting to be buried rather than cremated as was more usual in Roman society.

Right: The sacred ibis seems to have been bred specifically for the purpose of votive mummification. Vast numbers have been found in animal catacombs, notably at Saqqara.

Opposite: Glass fragment of a theatrical mask of the Greco-Roman period, showing a hetaira, *or courtesan. The Romans embraced numerous Egyptian practices and beliefs, including the calendar, which formed the basis for the modern Gregorian calendar. The temples at Dendera, Edfu, Kom Ombo, Esna, and Philae were completed during the Roman period, the names of emperors such as Trajan and Nero appearing in cartouches at these magnificent sites. A feature of these temples is the detailed hieroglyphs which describe in precise detail the words and movements to be used in ceremonial worship and ritual. The combination of breathtaking architecture and exact liturgy suggests that these temples were intended as a lasting testament to the Pharaonic era. When Egypt converted to Christianity in the fourth century AD, such temples were seen as bastions of paganism and many were defaced.*

The Egyptian Calendar

The Ancient Egyptians had a number of reference points for the measurement of time. They calculated —marginally erroneously—that it took 365 days for the sun to return to the same point on the southeastern horizon at winter solstice. A civil year was devised, consisting of 360 days plus five epagomenal days. The latter were said to be when the deities Osiris, Horus, Isis, Seth, and Nepthys were born and little was to be done in this period.

The civil calendar did have regard for one astronomical phenomenon, but not the movement of the sun. The annual heliacal rising of the dog star Sirius—July 19 by the later Julian calendar—was used to calculate the start of the new year. The 360 days were divided into twelve months, which were the basis for the three four-month seasons of the agricultural cycle. These were *akhet*, the period of inundation (July–October); *peret*, when sowing was done (November–February); and *shemu*, harvest time (March–June). As the solar year is 365.25 days, the agricultural and astronomical year were slightly misaligned; once they were out of phase it took 1460 years for the two to be synchronized naturally again.

The lunar cycle was also used for calculating certain festivals. Neither the astronomical nor civil calendar was helpful in marking the passage of time as there was no fixed starting point from which to measure. Regnal years were used for this purpose. For much of the Dynastic period a king's first year on the throne ended at the beginning of the new civil year, no matter how brief this period was. For even shorter periods of time the water clock or clepsydra was used. The earliest known example of this device dates from the Eighteenth Dynasty, c. 1500 BC.

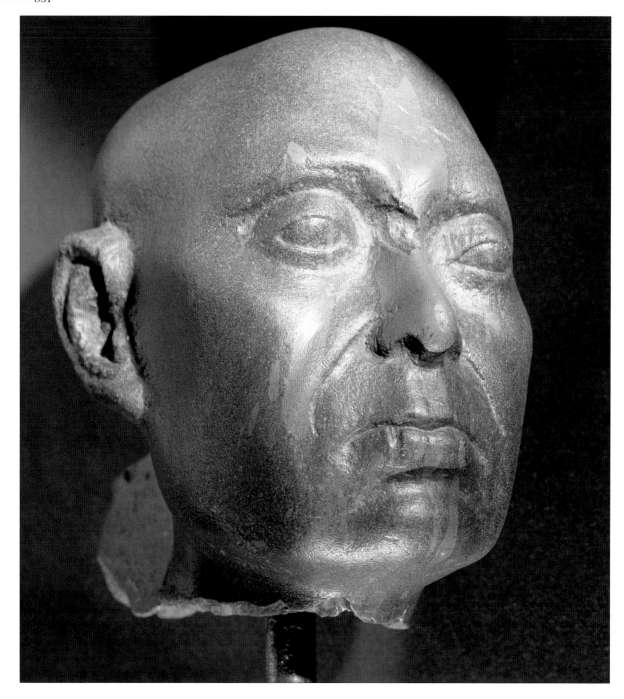

Opposite: The Romans adopted Egyptian burial practices but placed naturalistic portraits such as this onto the mummified corpse. By the second century AD the Egyptian tradition of placing funerary papyri with the body died out. When Renaissance Europe became interested in rediscovering the beliefs and customs of this great ancient civilization, much of the knowledge and understanding at the time was filtered through Rome. Scholars of the Middle Ages studied Egypt through Rome's perspective, which included many misinterpretations, for example, regarding the original role of the many Egyptian gods that were incorporated into the Roman pantheon.

Above: Head carved from green schist, dating from the Ptolemaic period. The influence of Pharaonic Egypt went far beyond Greece and Rome over the thousand years following the conquest by Macedonia. In fields as diverse as religion, art, architecture, literature, cinema, opera, mathematics, medicine, astronomy, and astrology, there are elements which have been informed or inspired by the world's first great civilization.

CHAPTER SIX

The Gods

Amun

Amun—"the Hidden One"—was an air deity who became a local Theban god, and thence head of the Egyptian pantheon. He is associated with a particular species of ram, one with downturned horns, an animal suggestive of pugnaciousness and virility. However,

Opposite: Anubis

Above: Amun

Amun is usually shown in human form, wearing a twin-plumed headdress incorporating a solar disk.

The founder of the Twelfth Dynasty, the usurper Amenemhat ("Amun is Supreme"), was instrumental in elevating Amun to the position of pre-eminent deity. He began work on the Temple of Karnak, which was extended and embellished by successive kings over the centuries.

Following the expulsion of the Hyksos invaders, c. 1550 BC, Thebes became the capital of the reunited land and Amun again enjoyed primacy. Later, he merged with Re to become the self-engendered creator god Amun-Re. It was the reaction to this all-consuming power and the advocacy of the Karnak priesthood that led to Amenhotep IV's shortlived experiment with Atenism. Under Tutankhamun Amun's position of pre-eminence was restored.

Although Thebes' influence waned during the Third Intermediate period, the cult of Amun continued to flourish: the Twenty-fifth Dynasty Kushite kings revered and promoted a god they believed originated in Nubia; Alexander the Great gained legitimacy by being accorded the title Son of Amun and thus the rightful inheritor of the throne; and Amun was worshiped throughout the Greco-Roman period, albeit under different names.

Anubis

Jackal-headed god of the dead and embalming. Jackals were common scavengers around cemeteries, and Egyptians revered them by way of appeasement, fearing the desecration of graves. Before Osiris became king of the Underworld, Anubis was Judge of the Dead. Thereafter Anubis was accommodated in the judgment proceedings as the bastard son of Osiris and Nephthys. He supervised the Weighing of the Heart ceremony, which took place before Osiris, and was the custodian of the dead on their journey to the afterlife.

Anubis' flesh was black, a color associated with regeneration as the dark silt deposits left by the annual inundation breathed new life into the soil. Anubis' skin was thus a symbol of rebirth rather than decay.

At first Anubis was exclusively concerned with the burial rites of pharaohs, but became a god of the dead for all Egyptians as funereal rituals underwent a democratization process. Priests carrying out embalming procedures wore jackal-headed masks to resemble Anubis.

Aten

The Aten was a solar deity represented by a simple disk, a purer form of sun worship than that which attended Re. The rise in the cult of the Aten was inextricably linked to the fortunes of the New Kingdom ruler Amenhotep IV,

Above: Aten

before which time it was merely a minor deity. In a move that was politically as much as theologically inspired, Amenhotep IV promoted the Aten to the exclusion of all other gods, who were ultimately proscribed. In around the fifth year of his reign the king changed his name from Amenhotep—"Amun is Content," to Akhenaten—"Glorious is the Aten." The royal court moved to a virgin site untainted by past traditions, near modern Tell el-Amarna. The new capital was named Akhetaten—"Horizon of the Aten."

Atenism was exclusive to the royal family; ordinary Egyptians could worship the Aten and receive its munificence only through the king, his queen, Nefertiti, and their children. This exclusivity was reinforced by the iconography of the period, where the king and his family were shown bathed in the rays emanating from the sun's disk. At the extremities of these rays were hands, some of which held the *ankh*, or sign of life.

The new theological order did not capture the imagination of Egyptians beyond Akhetaten, and even within the royal precinct there was soon disquiet. Under Akhenaten's successor, Smenkhare, the experiment was halted, and the return to the established order was completed during the reign of the boy-king Tutankhamun.

Atum

According to the Heliopolitan creation myth, Atum ("the All") appeared on the primeval mound which rose from the chaotic waters that covered the earth. The self-engendered god then produced Shu and Tefnut from his bodily fluids—which some versions interpret as sneezing, others as masturbation. Shu and Tefnut procreated to produce Geb and Nut, whose four offspring created a group of nine gods across four generations. Atum was at the head of this group, collectively known as the Ennead.

Atum merged with Re, a later Heliopolitan deity, to form the supreme solar–creator god Atum-Re. During the Old Kingdom Atum was believed to raise the dead king from his pyramid to take his place among the stars.

Atum was usually shown in human form, wearing the Double Crown of the Two Lands. Sovereignty over the whole of Egypt was thus used as a metaphor for lordship over the entire universe.

Bastet

The most popular feline goddess and a daughter of the Sun God, Bastet was originally depicted with the head of a lioness, with obvious connotations of aggressiveness and ferocity. Over time she became associated with the domesticated species, and thenceforward was shown as a cat-headed woman.

Above: Bastet was closely associated with cats which often featured in the wall paintings of private tombs during the Middle Kingdom.

Above: Bes

Bastet now assumed a maternal, protective role, which was often stressed by portraying her surrounded by kittens. However, cats were highly regarded as hunters, and in particular as killers of snakes, and so Bastet had both a gentle and ferocious aspect. Her cult center was the delta town of Per-Bastet, which became Bubastis when the area fell under Greece's sphere of influence. This was the site of the Temple of Bastet, the construction of which was begun during the reign of the Fourth Dynasty kings Khufu and Khafre. Here an annual festival took place, where there was boisterous merry-making. Large numbers of mummified cats have been discovered in special cemeteries in this region— modern Tell Basta—indicating the reverence the Egyptians held for these sacred animals.

Bes

Despite the grotesque appearance of this dwarf god, he was a benevolent deity, protector of pregnant women and children. Usually shown with a lion's mane, protruding tongue, tail, and long penis, Bes's role was to scare away evil forces which might threaten those in his care.

His consort was Taweret, who was depicted as a pregnant hippopotamus. Unlike the male of the species, which was regarded as a force for evil and bringer of chaos, the female hippopotamus was praised for its fecundity. Even so, like Bes, Taweret had a ferocious appearance which helped her fulfil her protective role. Both were extremely popular household deities.

Hathor

The Egyptian pantheon included a number of bovine goddesses, as cows were revered for their fertility and association with motherhood. Hathor was the most important of this group. She was depicted as either a cow or a woman with a cow's head, often with a solar disk between her horns. She was also a sky goddess, perceived as a gigantic cow straddling the earth, her legs indicating the cardinal compass points.

Hathor's image appears on the Narmer Palette, showing that she was an important deity by the time Egypt was unified c. 3100 BC.

She was a multifaceted deity. As one of the Eyes of Re she had a vengeful, destructive aspect. According to one myth, Hathor was sent by Re to teach a lesson to those who had been found conspiring against him. Assuming lioness form, she carried out her task with such gusto that the Sun God was forced to make her drunk in order to save mankind from total destruction. Hathor's association with alcohol was derived from this story.

Despite this retributive aspect, Hathor was mostly

Ancient Egypt

Above: Hathor

Above: Horus

identified with earthly pleasures: beauty, music, and love. She was often depicted on the handles of mirrors, which were used to apply makeup, and was particularly associated with the sistrum, a rattle-like instrument.

Hathor was also a fertility goddess. She was regarded as the divine mother of the reigning king, although this was a role she shared with other goddesses. Kings were depicted suckling from her udders. Hathor protected queens during pregnancy and childbirth, and after delivery her duties included that of royal nurse.

Hathor also had a funerary aspect. One of the epithets applied to her was "Lady of the West," the direction of the setting sun. She was believed to protect the sun during the hours of darkness, allowing it to begin its journey anew at dawn. All Egyptians sought similar protection on their journey to the afterlife.

Horus

The falcon god Horus was associated with kingship from the beginning of the Dynastic period. He was

not the only deity represented in the form of a hawk, but over time the others were either displaced or assimilated within the persona of Horus, around whom many myths grew. As the son of Isis, Horus engaged in a long struggle to defeat the evil Seth, murderer of his father Osiris. At first Re chose the experience of Seth over Horus's immaturity, and the latter is sometimes depicted as a child with the sidelock of youth. One account of the nephew–uncle battle describes a harpoon fight, in which both Horus and Seth are wounded. Isis helps her son, but also assists her evil brother Seth when he is struck. Enraged, Horus chops off his mother's head and disappears into the mountains. Isis, magically healed by Re, forgives her son. Seth pursues Horus and gouges out his eyes, but his sight is restored by Hathor. The "Wadjet" or "healed" eye became one of the powerful symbols of protection, often painted on coffins or used in amulet form.

After a heated exchange of letters between Re and Osiris, now king of the Underworld, Horus was granted the throne. The reigning Egyptian king was regarded as

Above: Isis and Horus

Above: Khepri

the living Horus, while deceased rulers were associated with Osiris. The mythology of the Ennead was used as a means of legitimizing succession to the throne. Whoever presided over the burial of the previous ruler was believed to be acting as Horus, irrespective of whether there was a blood tie between himself and the dead king.

Isis

A goddess of obscure origin, Isis became the divine mother of the reigning king by virtue of her place in the Heliopolitan Ennead. Isis was the daughter of Geb and Nut and sister-wife of King Osiris. Her valiant efforts in trying to restore her murdered husband to life, together with the lengths she went to in protecting her son, Horus, made Isis the archetypal loyal wife and devoted mother. She was sometimes depicted with wings, a reference to the fact that she changed herself into a kite and hovered over Osiris in an effort to breathe new life into him. During the New Kingdom Isis was often represented as a cow goddess, an animal associated with fecundity and a nurturing role. Many reliefs and statuettes show Isis suckling the infant Horus.

Isis merged with several other gods during the Late period. Her cult spread beyond Egypt's shores, and to many parts of the Roman Empire during Rome's period of dominion. Temples to Isis were erected in Rome itself, and her popularity rivaled that of the traditional Roman pantheon. She was revered and worshiped long after Egypt had converted to Christianity.

Khepri

A creator god manifested in the form of the scarab or dung beetle. This creature was thought to be self-generated, a belief which had natural resonance with the Egyptian view of creation. Also, the image of the dung beetle pushing its spherical pellet along was a ready symbol of the sun being propelled through the sky.

Khepri, whose literal meaning is "He who is coming into being," was usually depicted with a scarab's head

Above: Khnum, Hathor and Horus

atop a human body. Just as the sun underwent a process of daily renewal, so the scarab came to symbolize rebirth. Scarabs were commonly used in amulet form in burial rituals, often placed within the wrappings of a mummified body, particularly over the heart. Inscribed stone scarabs were also used for making public declarations and recording notable achievements.

Khnum

Ram-headed creator god whose cult center was the island of Elephantine, where the Egyptians believed the flood waters began their surge. Khnum was thus closely associated with the annual inundation, and thus the fertility of the land.

According to the Elephantine creation myth, Khnum molded the gods and all living things on his potter's wheel. Each person fashioned was allotted a certain lifespan, a concept which came to be regarded more generally as fate. After years of toil, Khnum is said to have wearied of his task. He thus placed a potter's wheel within every female womb so that procreation could occur independently.

The Egyptian word for "ram" was *ba*, the term applied to an individual's nonphysical attributes, loosely akin to "personality." Khnum was regarded as the *ba* of the Sun God Re, who was depicted with a ram's head as he traveled through the netherworld in his solar barque.

Khonsu

Khonsu was a Theban deity, believed there—though not universally—to be the son of Amun and Mut. He was usually depicted as a mummiform youth holding a crook and flail, symbols of kingship. He wears the sidelock of youth, and a headdress incorporating images of both a crescent and full moon. As a lunar deity, Khonsu was naturally associated with time and the calendar; his very name translates as "wanderer," suggesting his own journey across the skies.

Khonsu was also identified with healing. When Ptolemy Philopator (221–205 BC) became seriously ill, he appealed not to the Greek gods of his heritage but to Khonsu. He recovered completely, and bestowed upon himself the title "Beloved of Khonsu who protects His Majesty and drives away evil spirits."

Maat

The goddess of truth and justice, Maat was usually shown as a seated figure with an ostrich feather on her head. In the Weighing of the Heart ceremony a feather was used to establish whether the dead could pass into the Underworld. If the misdeeds of the heart outweighed the feather of Maat, then access to the afterlife was denied. In practice this appears to have been a rare occurrence, Anubis often tipping the balance to give a favorable outcome.

The goddess Maat also stood for the wider concept of order and harmony, the natural equilibrium of the universe which was established at the point of creation, and the maintenance of which was one of the prime duties of the reigning pharaoh. Conversely, chaos in any form was abhorrent to the Egyptians. Animals such as the crocodile and male hippopotamus were regarded as a threat to order, and were hunted as evil-doers. Similarly, the New Kingdom queen Hatshepsut, who declared herself pharaoh, was later expunged from king-lists since her self-aggrandizement was seen as contrary to the principles of *maat*.

Min

A fertility god usually depicted as a semi-mummiform male figure wearing a twin-plumed headdress. Min was

Below: Min

Below: The Pharaoh Mentuhotep II, one of four rulers particularly associated with the god Montu.

associated with the bull, with its obvious connotations of virility. He thus figured prominently in the *sed* festival, one of whose aims was reaffirmation of the king's potency. The fecundity of the land underpinned Egypt's economic base, and as such harvest time was a period of great rejoicing. These celebrations included the Festival of the Coming Forth of Min, when statues of the god were brought out from the temples. During the New Kingdom the pre-eminent deity Amun was worshiped in ithyphallic form as Min, notably at the Temple of Luxor.

Montu

Falcon-headed god, often shown with a headdress consisting of a solar disk surmounted by twin plumes. Montu rose to prominence during the Eleventh Dynasty as patron deity of four kings with the birth name Mentuhotep—"Montu is satisfied." It was around the same time that he became identified as a warrior-god. Montu was a Theban deity, with a temple dedicated to him within the Karnak complex. During the Twelfth Dynasty he was overshadowed by another Theban god, Amun, and his position in the pantheon diminished, despite merging with Re to form Montu-Re. However, the great warrior-kings of the New Kingdom continued to invoke Montu's name when they went on the conquest trail.

Mut

In the Predynastic era Mut was a vulture goddess, possibly the original Theban deity. During the Pharaonic period she was depicted in human form with a vulture headdress. When Amun rose to become king of the gods, Mut was installed as his divine consort. The temple dedicated to Mut at Karnak is linked to the Temple of Amun by a row of ramheaded sphinxes.

One of the meanings of "Mut" is "mother," indicative of her maternal aspect. The image of the outstretched vulture's wings was used to stress her protective role. Mut was divine mother to the reigning king, although this role was shared with other goddesses. She also had a ferocious aspect as one of the Eyes of Re, the goddesses who wreaked vengeance on those who had incurred the wrath of the Sun God.

Right: Neith
Opposite: Mut

Above: Nut

Neith had a maternal aspect, for which she was associated with the cow. She was also a funerary deity. Along with Isis, Nephthys, and Serket, she helped the deities known as the Four Sons of Horus to protect the sarcophagus and canopic jars. Neith's particular association was with the jackal-headed Duamutef, whose responsibility was to guard the canopic jar containing the intestines.

Neith enjoyed favored status during the Twenty-sixth Dynasty, whose kings ruled from Sais.

Nekhbet

Vulture goddess who was the tutelary deity of Upper Egypt, and thus the counterpart of Wadjet. "The Two Ladies," which became part of the royal titulary in the early Dynastic era, referred to Nekhbet and Wadjet, reinforcing the concept of dominion over the entire land.

In the Predynastic period Nekhbet was regarded as a protector of the king of Upper Egypt, and this role continued post-unification. To this end pectorals worn by the king were often in vulture form. In her claws the goddess often held the hieroglyphic *shen* sign, meaning "to encircle"; this suggested both eternity and that the king had sovereignty over all that the sun's journey encompassed.

The uraeus worn by the king offered protection in the form of a rearing cobra, and also confirmed the position of the wearer as ruler over Upper and Lower Egypt. In this instance Nekhbet, like Wadjet, could be depicted in cobra form.

Nephthys

Nephthys was an obscure goddess who gained importance as a member of the Ennead, the nine deities spanning four generations who provided the dramatis personae for the Heliopolitan creation myth. Nephthys was sister-wife of the evil Seth, who murdered their brother Osiris out of jealousy. She helped Isis collect the dismembered body parts of Osiris, and the two sisters were chief mourners at his burial. During the Dynastic era Nephthys assumed the role of protector of the dead. She was one of the goddesses who assisted the Four Sons of Horus in protecting the sarcophagus and canopic jars. She stood guard over the baboon-headed god Hapy, who in turn watched over the head of the coffin. This equated to the north, the sarcophagus being aligned with the cardinal points of the compass. Nephthys and Hapy also had responsibility for the canopic jar containing the lungs.

Neith

A multifaceted deity, Neith was a creator goddess, said to have emerged from the primeval waters to create light and the other deities. One version of the story has it that Neith then departed for the delta town of Sais, leaving the god Khnum to continue her work, fashioning all living things on his potter's wheel. Sais was Neith's cult center, and she was usually shown wearing the Red Crown of Lower Egypt.

From the Early Dynastic period Neith was also regarded as a goddess of war, her emblems being the shield and bow. Later, she was seen as consort to the god Seth, and mother of the crocodile god, Sobek.

Nut

The sky goddess, believed to swallow the sun each evening and give birth to it at the dawn of every day. Like Hathor, with whom she is closely associated, Nut was believed to straddle the earth in the form of a cow, her legs indicating the cardinal points of the compass. It was Re who commanded Nut to ascend to the heavens, and the blue dress she wore to do the Sun God's bidding gave the sky its color. He was able to rest on Nut's back during his daytime journey through the skies.

According to the Heliopolitan creation myth, Nut was the sister-wife of the earth god Geb. She gave birth to five children, including Osiris, whose murder by his evil brother Seth was ultimately avenged by his son Horus. A family rift had resulted in Nut being cursed and prevented from giving birth on the 360 days of the Egyptian year. Nut won five extra days in a game of dice from her lover Thoth, god of time. This story was used to account for the five epagomenal days through which the Egyptians attempted to synchronize the lunar and solar cycles.

Below: Osiris

Osiris

Osiris was said to have been a beneficent Egyptian king who was betrayed and murdered by his jealous brother, Seth. In shades of the Cinderella story, Seth invited the assembled guests at a banquet to lie in an ornate chest, and whomsoever it fitted would be able to keep it. The chest had been made with Osiris in mind, and when the king lay inside, the conspirators nailed it shut and threw it in the Nile. The chest washed up on the Lebanese coast, where a tamarisk tree sprouted and enclosed it. The local king ordered the tree to be chopped down and the trunk used as a pillar within his palace. Osiris's sister-wife Isis freed her husband's body and returned to Egypt. Her attempts to hide Osiris failed as he was discovered by Seth, who dismembered the king's body and scattered the parts throughout the land. Helped by Nephthys, her sister and sister-wife to Seth, Isis collected all the pieces save for the penis, which was eaten by a fish after being thrown into the Nile. With the aid of Anubis and Thoth the body was reassembled and swathed in bandages—the first mummified body. Isis attempted to breathe life into Osiris by transforming herself into a kite and beating her wings. This failed, and instead of reclaiming the Egyptian throne Osiris became king of the Underworld.

Egypt's kings replicated the Osiris legend in the hope that they too would be reborn in the afterlife. This included the presence of a priest wearing the jackal-headed mask of Anubis, and the entire embalming and mummification processes. During the Old Kingdom the deceased king was identified with Osiris. As funerary religion became democratized, so all Egyptians sought salvation by the same means. This brought with it the importance of Abydos—Osiris's cult center—as a pilgrimage site. Egyptians regarded it as vital to visit Abydos either during their lifetime or postmortem. The latter could be achieved either by having the coffin taken there, or by the use of boat models, which were included in the funerary goods for that purpose.

Osiris was depicted in human form, with a close fitting shroud through which his hands protruded; these hold the crook and flail, symbols of kingship. He is typically shown wearing the White Crown of Upper Egypt flanked by ostrich feathers. Osiris's skin is sometimes green, the color of vegetation, or black, the color of the rich Nile silt deposits; both symbolize regeneration.

Ptah

Ptah was the creator god of Memphis, Egypt's first capital following the country's unification c. 3100 BC. Unlike Atum, from whose bodily fluids all life emerged, Ptah created the world by thought and utterance, a more cerebral process. The very fact that the Memphite creation myth was more intellectual, less concrete than the Heliopolitan tradition, meant that it was never warmly embraced by ordinary Egyptians. Accordingly, Ptah's importance waned during the Old Kingdom, when Re gained prominence and Osiris also enjoyed elevated status in the pantheon. Ptah's position was further undermined when Memphis lost its position as capital. However, his aspect as patron deity of crafts and craftsmen was unaffected.

By the Middle Kingdom Ptah had merged with another Memphite god, the hawkheaded funerary deity Sokar, and during the Late period Osiris was also incorporated to form Ptah-Sokar-Osiris. Wooden figures of this composite deity were often included in the funerary equipment of the period.

Ptah was usually depicted as a mummiform figure, with hands protruding through the bandages. These held a staff representing the was sceptre and *djed* pillar, symbols of dominion and stability respectively. The crook and flail, and the *ankh* also appeared in the iconography. In animal form Ptah was worshiped as a bull. This creature, synonymous with virility, was sacred in Memphis before Ptah's emergence as a creator god. Over time the two became linked, and one bull was selected to be the incarnation of Ptah and act as his herald. The Apis Bull was kept in a stall near the Temple of Ptah, attracting visits from those who wanted to make offerings or undertake an oracular consultation.

Re

Re was the pre-eminent solar deity, whose cult center was Heliopolis. During the Old Kingdom his cult spread throughout the land, and by the Fourth Dynasty, kings began to include "Son of Re" in the royal titulary. The Step Pyramid was devised as a stairway by which the king could join Re in his journey through the sky. Later straight-sided pyramids were a physical representation of the sun's rays falling on the earth, and thus the connection between kingship and Re was maintained, as it was for the entire Pharaonic era.

Fifth Dynasty kings constructed solar temples as well as pyramids, marking Re's elevation to the position of Egypt's state god. The centerpiece of these temples was the obelisk, symbol of the Sun God since Predynastic times. Many were removed, either by conquest or as a gift offering. These included Cleopatra's Needle, the name given to two obelisks, one of which was moved to London's Thames Embankment in 1878, the other to New York's Central Park two years later.

Re traveled through the daytime skies in his solar barque. At night he voyaged through the Underworld or,

Above: A depiction of the union of the gods Ra and Osiris in the guise of a ram-headed mummy.

in some versions of the myth, was swallowed by the sky goddess Nut and reborn with each new dawn.

Along with the Nile, the sun was the great life-giving force. This made Re a potent god both in his own right, and, through syncretism, when he was merged with other deities. He was allied with Horus to form Re-Horakhty, with Montu to form Montu-Re, and with Amun to form Amun-Re. He also combined with Atum to form the creator god Atum-Re. In this aspect he was believed to have created the gods and mankind from his bodily fluids. Everything else he created simply by the act of naming it.

The cult of Re was specifically for Egyptian royalty; ordinary Egyptians worshiped the Sun God only indirectly. With the decline in royal authority at the end of the Old Kingdom and the democratization of funerary

rituals, Egyptians turned to Osiris for their personal salvation. Re remained an important member of the pantheon but never regained the pre-eminence he enjoyed during the Old Kingdom.

Sekhmet

A lioness goddess whose name—"Powerful One"—suggests the aggressiveness which was her foremost aspect. She was a goddess of war, helping kings to vanquish their foe; she was also one of the Eyes of Re, those who wrought vengeance on enemies of the Sun God, who was her father.

Sekhmet, who was usually depicted in female form with the head of a lioness, was a Memphite goddess, consort of that city's creator god Ptah. During the New Kingdom, Thebes and the Theban deities rose to prominence, and Sekhmet came to be seen as a manifestation of her counterpart there: Mut, wife of Amun.

Despite her ferocious aspect, Sekhmet was also associated with healing. This may have been because the concept of driving illness from the body was regarded as an apposite task for a warrior-goddess.

Left: Sekhmet
Below: Seth

Seth

One of the nine members of the Heliopolitan Ennead, Seth represented chaos and evil. He was usually depicted as an imaginary doglike animal with a long snout and forked tail. Actual creatures with which Seth was associated included the pig—which was regarded as unclean—and those who posed a threat to order, such as the crocodile, hippopotamus, and snake. Seth was also linked with the desert, which for geographical reasons the Egyptians equated with foreign lands, and thus a potential source of danger. There were beneficent aspects to Seth's character. As god of the nighttime sky he traveled with Re in his solar barque, and protected the Sun God from attack by the serpent Apophis, a myth which is thought to be the template for the George and the dragon story of the Christian tradition. However, despite this laudable aspect, Seth was mostly associated with dark forces, the antithesis of *maat*.

According to legend, a jealous Seth murdered his brother, the benevolent Egyptian king, Osiris. He then engaged in a protracted battle with his nephew Horus, son of Osiris and Isis. One account describes how Seth tried to trick Horus into engaging in a homosexual act, the worst indignity a victor could inflict on his beaten enemy. Through this he hoped the gods would deride Horus and favor him in their dispute. But Horus turned the tables on his uncle, and a furious Seth then challenged Horus to a sea race in stone boats. Horus again got the better of him, coating his wooden vessel with gypsum. The battle between the two is said to have lasted some eighty years,

Horus emerging the winner and claiming the Egyptian throne.

The Egyptian concept of duality required that *maat*—the harmonious working of the universe—could only be maintained by the existence of opposing forces, and Seth was important as a figure representing disorder.

Thoth

The Egyptians mourned the loss of the life-giving sun over the western horizon. It is said that Re commanded Thoth to provide light in the sun's absence, and the moon was thus formed. As a lunar deity Thoth was naturally associated with time and the calendar.

Thoth was worshiped in ibis or baboon form, and often depicted holding a reed pen. He was scribe to the

Left Thoth (in baboon form)
Above: Thoth (in ibis form)

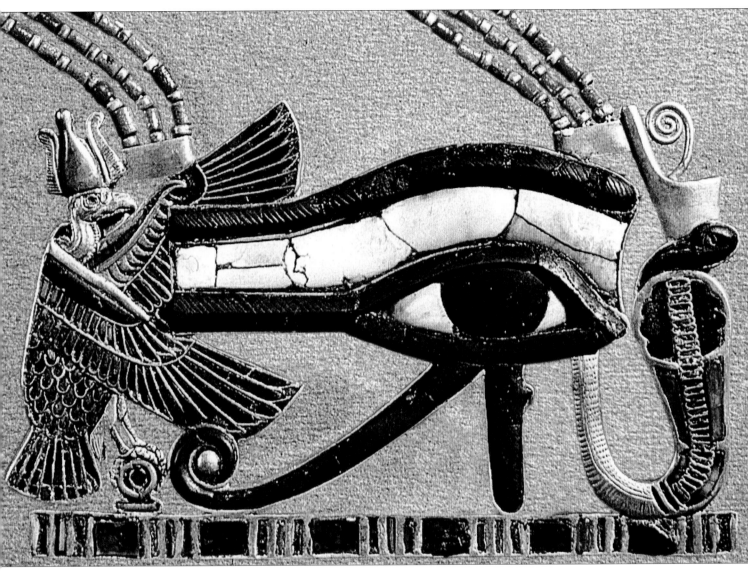

Above: Wadjet

gods, and also official recorder at the Weighing of the Heart ceremony. Thoth was also god of wisdom. He was believed to have devised hieroglyphic writing, and to have written forty-two books containing all the wisdom of the entire world.

Wadjet

In Predynastic times Wadjet was worshiped in cobra form in the delta region. She became tutelary goddess of Lower Egypt and was usually depicted wearing the Red Crown, symbol of Egypt's northern domain. Her southern counterpart was Nekhbet, and post-unification coronation images show the king receiving the Red and White Crowns, from Wadjet and Nekhbet respectively. In such scenes Wadjet appears in female form, but at other times she was depicted as a rearing cobra, a creature which to the Egyptians symbolized sovereignty.

According to myth, Wadjet guarded the infant Horus when Isis was forced to leave him unattended on the island of Khemmis. Horus grew to triumph over the evil Seth and claim the throne that had belonged to his father, Osiris. As all pharaohs were regarded as the living Horus, Wadjet was seen as the king's protector. The manifestation of this role was in the uraeus, which formed part of the royal headdress. Wadjet is poised, ready to strike at any potential enemy of the pharaoh. The uraeus sometimes incorporated Nekhbet, who was depicted either in vulture or cobra form. This item of royal regalia thus had a protective function and also established the wearer as having dominion over both Upper and Lower Egypt.

Index

Bibliography

The Complete Tutankhamun
Nicholas Reeves Thames & Hudson

Tutankhamen: The Life and Death of a Boy King
Christine el Mahdy/Headline

The British Museum Book of Ancient Egypt
Ed by Stephen Quirke & Jeffrey Spencer

Ancient Egypt: The Great Discoveries
Nicholas Reeves/Thames & Hudson

Egypt: The World of the Pharaohs
Ed by Regine Schulz & Matthias Seidel/Konemann

British Museum Dictionary of Ancient Egypt
Ian Shaw and Paul Nicholson/BCA

Egypt: The Splendours of an Ancient Civilization
Alberto Sillotti/Thames & Hudson

Ancient Egypt
Lorna Oakes & Lucia Gahlin/Hermes House

Gods of Ancient Egypt
B Watterson /Sutton Publishing

Discovering Ancient Egypt
Rosalie David/Michael O'Mara Books Ltd

Ancient Egyptians
Anton Gill/HarperCollins

Egyptology
James Putnam/Grange Books

Ramesses: The Great Warrior and Builder
Bernadette Menu/Thames & Hudson

Akhenaten's Egypt
Angela P. Thomas/Shire Publications Ltd

The Pharaohs Master Builders
Henri Stierlin/Terrail

Picture Acknowledgements

All photographs except the following © Werner Forman Archive

6, 11(tp), 38-39, 82, 84,92, 132,133, 142, 143, 150-151, 152-153, 155(t and bl), 156-157, 158-159, 161, 164, 165, 166, 167, 174, 176, 177, 178-179 © Dr E Strouhal

Artefacts photographed in the following institutions: Ariadne Gallery, New York 237(bt): Ashmolean Museum, Oxford 18, 22: British Museum, London 21, 56, 63, 64, 76, 106(bt), 168(tp), 168(bt), 168(tp), 169, 170-171, 180 (tp), 184, 208-209, 210-211: Brooklyn Museum NY 118, 126(tp): Cheops Barque Museum 36: Christie's London 126(bt), 192 (bt,lf), 196, 198, 229(t and b), 230, 231, 225(b), 247(l), 248(b): Collection of George Ortiz Vandoeuvres 80: Antiquarians Gallery 201: Daedallus Gallery, NY 202: Detroit Institute of Art 127: Egyptian Museum, Berlin 70(bt), 120, 123, 134, 175(tp): Egyptian Museum, Cairo 16, 23, 26, 27, 32,33 (bt), 37(t), 46, 47(lf), 47 (rt), 48(tp), 48(bt), 49(bt), 54, 55, 57(tp), 60, 69 (tp), 66, 81, 70 (tp),72 (tp), 72(bt), 88, 96(bt), 99, 102, 115, 116, 117, 119, 136/7 138, 144/5, 146, 149(tp and bt), 186/7,191(bt), 194, 197, 200, 203, 206 (tp lt), 206 (tp rt), 206 (bt), 207, 175(bt), 193, 212(tp), 212 (bt),213, 226-227, 235, 249, 129 (tp), 138, 139, 140, 141,147(l and r), 148, 247(r): Egyptian Museum, Turin 59(tp), 59(bt),67, 85, 135, 191(tp): Fitzwilliam Museum, Cambridge 77(tp), 214, 215: Graeco-Roman Museum, Alexandria Egypt 205: Gulbenkian Museum, Lisbon 232: J Paul Getty Museum Malibu 233: John Kluge Collection, Virginia 199: Louvre, Paris 28, 29, 43, 74(tp), 125, 188(bt), 189, 217: Luxor Museum 242: Metropolitan Museum of Art, NY 68, 69 (bt), 77 (bt), 71, 73, 75, 124(tp), 182, 188(tp and bt), 192(tp): Museum Of Fine Arts Boston 228: Nicholas Reeves, London 216: Ny Carlsberg Glyptotek, Copenhagen 33 (tp), 42, 79: Private Collection 185: Royal Museum of Art & History Brussels 180 (bt), 181, 183: Royal Scottish Museum, Edinburgh 65: Schimmel Collection, NY 114, 121, 122, 124(bt), 190: Schindler Collection NY 225(tp): St Louis Art Museum 87:

The publisher would like to thank Themis Halvantzi and Barbara Heller at the Werner Forman Archive for their help in producing this book.